BREAKING AND ENTERING

THE GRADUATE'S GUIDE TO MANAGEMENT CONSULTING

A complete guide to the consulting
industry and how to get in

By Zihao Xu

Published by Zedex Schumann Ltd

124 New Bond Street, London W1S 1DX

http://www.zedexschumann.com/

First edition published in 2013

http://www.breaking-entering.com/

Disclaimer: This book represents the knowledge I've collected over the years about the consulting recruitment process, and is based on my experience in London. I can in no way guarantee that the information presented is accurate, or will land you a job or even an interview at any firm whatsoever. Furthermore, all information presented in this book is the opinion, informed or otherwise, of the author. None of it is presented as fact. It would be nice if you didn't pirate this book. Thanks. Also GMAT is a registered trademark of the Graduate Management Admission Council, which was not involved in the writing of this book and does not endorse this book. All names of consulting firms are used only for reference, and do not imply any sort of endorsement.

"A man is a success if he gets up in the morning and goes to bed at night, and in between does what he wants to do"

- Bob Dylan

TABLE OF CONTENTS

PREFACE

Hello, dear reader, and welcome. I suppose it's good practice to start with a preface, to set the scene, and to answer any burning questions you may have.

WHAT'S THIS BOOK ALL ABOUT THEN?

You're either thinking about a career in consulting, or actively trying to break in. As far as I'm concerned, to have the best chance of landing a job at a top management consulting firm and succeeding once you're in, you need to exhibit two qualities:

- You know what the consulting experience really is, and that genuinely aligns with your long-term career aspirations, whether in consulting or otherwise

- You are the type of person a consulting firm wants to hire

The aim of this book is to deal with both these points. I start by introducing what management consulting is, what the work is like, what the life is like and what the career prospects are, without any of the spiel used by the firms themselves to try to entice you. Then the rest of the book goes on to explain what kind of person a consulting firm wants to hire, and how to become that person.

WHO ARE YOU?

My name is Zihao Xu. I emigrated with my parents to the UK from mainland China at the age of 5. After graduating with a BA in Economics and Management from the University of Oxford, I proceeded to enter the world of management consulting, where I have been working for over two and a half years, during which time I have reviewed hundreds of CVs and interviewed dozens of candidates.

WHY HAVE YOU WRITTEN THIS BOOK?

Almost immediately after I entered the world of management consulting I started receiving messages through friends, friends of friends, family, Facebook and LinkedIn connections, and the Oxford alumni network asking for advice on how to break into the industry. After about fifteen phone calls and Skype conversations that largely covered the same essential information, I decided to write a short primer on the recruitment process and how best to navigate it. I intended to send this to anyone else who got in touch, so they could go through and digest my basic message in their own time and formulate any additional questions.

That primer has evolved into this book. Having been through the rigorous recruiting process myself, I know that seeking employment in management consulting can be stressful and demoralising without the right guidance, and in my opinion the knowledge contained in this book ought to provide much of that guidance.

I suppose this book comprises things I wish I had known when I was going through the application process, and I think it would be very useful to anyone applying, or thinking about applying, to a management consulting firm. Finally, as far as I can tell, there is no other book like this currently on the market.

HOW IS THIS BOOK DIFFERENT?

This book is different in two ways.

Firstly, I've not yet come across a book that provides a one-stop shop for advice on getting into consulting, from thinking about whether consulting is right for you, to preparing your CV, to all stages of the interview and finally to how to succeed in your first weeks and months as a consultant. This book covers all of that.

Secondly, my approach is not just to give you tips and tricks that allow you to bluff your way through the interview process by learning the right answers. Your career is far too important for that. Getting hired by a management consulting firm is not about remembering the right answers, but about becoming the kind of person a consulting firm really wants to hire. Not merely appearing to be that kind of person, but actually becoming that person. Not only will you then have the best chance of getting hired, but you'll have the best chance of succeeding once you're in. This book tells you what characteristics you should embody to become the perfect candidate that consulting firms want working for them, and furthermore how to get the message across that you are said perfect candidate.

WHO IS THIS BOOK AIMED AT?

This book will be most useful to you if you are a university/college student/recent graduate applying/thinking about applying for a graduate entry position in a top consulting firm. That said, I believe a lot of the content is applicable to slightly more senior hires also.

WHICH ARE THE TOP CONSULTING FIRMS?

In London, McKinsey, Boston Consulting Group, and Bain are the big dogs of the industry, with Roland Berger, Oliver Wyman, OC&C and LEK representing the elite second tier. Then there are the consulting arms of the Big 4 accounting firms, as well as a whole host of boutiques such as PA Consulting, Javelin, Parthenon, etc. that are a bit smaller. It's well worth doing your research/talking with those in the industry about the differences between these firms.

As a graduate, I pretty much just made a list of these companies by size/prestige and went to the highest one on the list that made me an offer. However, once you join the industry, you realise that there are very big differences between them, and it's not necessarily the largest, most prestigious one that will be the best fit for you. In general, you can expect larger firms to offer more structured development and a more glamorous client list, but smaller firms are a lot more flexible. And that's not just a buzzword. As I write this text, I'm working three days per week as a consultant at one such smaller firm after serving just over two years full time. I'd eat my hat if anyone at the same level got to do this at one of the Big 3.

Choose wisely, young warrior.

CAN ANYONE WHO PUTS THEIR MIND TO IT GET IN?

No. Graduate positions in these firms are silly competitive. The year I received my offer, my firm hired five graduates out of a pool of more than thirteen hundred candidates. This year it was the same number of offers to more than two thousand candidates. To put that in perspective, when I was admitted to the University of Oxford, there were just 80 applications for the 5 places on my course at my college. There are fewer than 150 graduate places on offer every year at the top consulting firms in London.

Essentially, there are far more qualified candidates than places, and every year hundreds of candidates who would probably have done an excellent job will get rejected. Hence, you can use all the help you can get. That includes this book, and any other reputable book. It also includes asking any friends or family that work in consulting for help, and networking with those in the industry to get a leg up.

Sometimes it can be easier to get in after a few years working in another field - you'll probably be a little older than those at the same level who joined as a graduate, but you'll also have outside experience that is very valuable indeed.

DO I HAVE TO READ THIS BOOK COVER TO COVER?

It depends on who you are. If you already know exactly what management consulting entails and you're set on being a consultant, you can probably skip Part One. If you just want case interview practice, you can just read that part too. However, I recommend that you read the entire thing, and not just for my ego. The first part introduces some of the key characteristics of the industry and of the most successful candidates, while the second part tells you how to become that successful candidate. Unless you're already very well-versed in what it takes to be a successful consultant, then there's a good chance the second part of the book may lose you at times if you don't read the first.

Right - let's get started then!

PART 1

MANAGEMENT CONSULTING: A BRIEF INTRODUCTION

WHAT IS MANAGEMENT CONSULTING?

The role of a management consultant is to become your client's trusted advisor on all commercial issues. You do this by undertaking projects that can all be broadly described as performance improvement in some way or other. Whether it's helping your client to increase sales, streamline their supply chain or reduce overheads, you're ultimately assisting them in achieving their goals quicker and at a lower cost than they otherwise could. Or sometimes you're helping them define what their short-term goals ought to be in order to achieve their long-term ambitions. A management consultant is able to act as a guide in forming targets, plotting how to achieve them, and maintaining structure and discipline in implementation.

What do you bring to the table that the client doesn't already have? A structured approach, an independent opinion and a work ethic that cannot be matched by any client's internal team.

WHAT ARE THE PROJECTS LIKE?

Projects in management consulting are incredibly varied, both by industry and by function, which provides much of the appeal.

Industry

Unless you're joining a consultancy that puts you in an industry team immediately (and most don't), you'll be working in a very wide variety of industries; some of which you'll have heard of, some of which you won't have.

If all you've ever done is study and read business cases in textbooks, the first thing that will strike you when you join the world of consulting is the sheer number of industries and firms that are out there, all serving their customers and making money. There are niche firms serving niche roles in multi-billion pound industries you've never even thought about. And a lot of them want consulting services. So while you will serve blue chip consumer facing clients that all your friends and families will have heard of, chances are you'll also be doing work for very niche clients that work in very specialised and sometimes technical areas.

If you have a genuine passion for business, you will – like I was – be fascinated by all of these industries, how they fit in with each other, how they generate value in the world, and how they fit within the larger headline industries. For example, you know about cargo shipping, of course, and you probably are aware of shipping insurance. Well, there's an industry out there that provides technical staff to oversee that a shipping operation is following all the necessary procedures that the insurance underwriter demands for the operation's insurance to be valid. You might spend some time on a project looking into the industry that trains those technical staff. And if you're anything like me, you'll find it fascinating. With each of these industries you delve into, you're becoming a little more knowledgeable about how the world works. You'll come across funny little business models that intrigue you with their ingenuity. You'll be astounded by how often some of the same practices occur. Sometimes you may come across an industry that bores the socks off you. Whatever. You'll see everything.

Yes, you will end up working for that airline everyone you know flies with, and yes that company that makes the soft drink you love is probably a client, and working for them will be every bit as exciting as you expect it to be. The point I'm making is that not all clients are that big, famous or glamorous. In fact, most aren't. And you'll love those smaller clients, too. Or hate them just as much as you hate the bigger ones for being so woefully inefficient that you have to work 15-hour days to help improve them. If you're someone who is genuinely passionate about business, the size of the client shouldn't matter to you and you should be excited all the same. If it does matter to you, then you're better off not applying to consulting. You wouldn't enjoy it, and someone more passionate would be better at it anyway.

Function

You want to join consulting because you want to deal with the big issues, right? You want to help some conglomerate navigate the tempestuous seas of international growth. That'll be something to brag about. It's fine – I wanted to, too. But get this: Not every project you work on will be blue-sky thinking, highly strategic or world shaping. Think about it this way: Out of the FTSE 100, how many companies are making 5-year strategy plans every year? How many do you think hire consultants? Of the ones that do, what do you think are the chances that they'll hire your firm, and that you'll be the chump who gets to work on it? So you see, there's just not that much of that kind of business going around.

Consulting companies engage in so much more than just high-level strategic issues. At first I found this somewhat disillusioning. I had worked hard at school and at university, so therefore I should obviously be let loose to advise the overall strategic direction at a major corporation. Heck, I should be dictating strategy at EVERY major corporation. It's as if they didn't realise I had a university degree! Alas, my 21-year-old self was quickly put in his place. Consulting companies advise on a wide variety of functional issues, from the strategic to the downright dirty. I know some guys whose work made it into the Financial Times. I also know some guys who were shouting at factory workers in India for four months straight. The reason consultancies deal with all of these issues is because all of these issues are problems clients deal with when running a business. You can't run a business just by making slideshows about strategy all day long. So not only do you have to get used to it, I advise you to learn to love it, if you don't already.

Most consulting projects can be classified into one of the following areas, which pretty much all consultancies engage in:

Strategic

These are the classic consulting projects most graduates think of when management consulting is mentioned. They are the sexy, high level projects that consultancies advertise to candidates to try to attract them. We're talking 5-year plans, market entry strategies, product portfolio assessments and anything else that has an impact on a company's overall direction and the businesses it's involved in. Anecdotally, the bigger, more prestigious firms may get slightly more of this type of business, but I don't know with any level of academic rigour. These projects can be based either at the client site or in the consultant's office, but usually a mixture of both.

Operational

Operational projects are the ones where you're playing with the meat and bones of how a company makes and spends its money. You will be based at the client site and getting very intimate with how it runs. Projects tend to revolve around cost reduction, process design, supply chain strategy, production efficiency, etc. Anything that makes a process that's already in place run more smoothly. These tend to be longer projects - anywhere from 2 to 6 months, sometimes longer. You'll spend less time presenting to the client and more time on the production line making tangible things actually happen. Which is cool.

Restructuring

The client is in trouble. They've realised that in a month's time they'll no longer be able to pay their creditors. In you swoop to save the day. These projects are very busy and very stressful, because the stakes are high. If you fail, the company goes under and a lot of people lose their jobs. You'll most likely be spending your time trying to come up with a reasonable business plan to present to creditors and banks that gives them enough confidence to provide the client with a bit more cash to turn itself around.

Market Assessment/Due Diligence

These projects generally support M&A transactions. When a company or private equity firm wants to purchase an asset, they hire consultancies to check that the asset is performing at the level management says it is. Sometimes they need to prove to the bank they're borrowing from that the asset is a sound investment. Sometimes you'll be hired by the sell-side bank to prepare the vendor due diligence document. Whichever side you're working for, the project will be largely similar - a few weeks researching the market, the competitors, the customer landscape, suppliers, technological trends and internal company operations to try to find out if the asset is a sound investment.

Anything in between/other

Consulting firms are probably the most flexible of all professional services, and there are a multitude of projects that don't really fall under the above categories. Pricing, market attack, scenario planning, brand management, etc. A whole host of stuff. Also, every once in a while something a little out of the ordinary will come along. Enjoy it.

So you get the idea. You'll work in loads of industries and in all kinds of functions. Pretty neat. You will not get a similar breadth of experience in any other industry. In the world. However, just bear in mind that what each individual office does can vary greatly, and their activities are often quite opaque to candidates trying to get into the industry. Reach out to as many consultants as you can through personal networks, your university network and online to try to get an idea about what exactly it is you're applying to join.

HOW'S THE LIFESTYLE?

It varies from not great to pretty horrific, in roughly a Chi-Squared distribution. That's if you benchmark it against having a pretty chilled life where you get to do stuff every evening after work. If you benchmark against comparable alternative professional services jobs you might get instead, then it's pretty standard. There are two aspects to the lifestyle we need to deal with: the workload and the travel.

Firstly, the travel. It's not as glamorous as a lot of people think. But then again the majority of it isn't as bad as a lot of the stories out there, either. You might get to fly to Paris, but chances are you'll spend a lot of your time at the airport, your hotel and the client site, and traveling between the three. If you're based away from home on a long term project, you'll often have the choice between flying home from Friday to Sunday or spending the same amount on a flight anywhere you like. Or you might be able to fly a friend/partner out to see you. A lot of firms follow a pattern of being based at the client site Monday to Thursday and coming back to the office on Fridays. But there's a lot of variance in this depending on which firm you're with, and the particular project you're on.

Some people love the jet-setting - usually young, single men. Others hate being away from home so often and living out of a suitcase for so long. Remember, though, that sometimes you might not see any travel at all for a few projects, so it really is difficult to say.

In terms of workload, you can expect to average 11-12 hour days. And it will vary a bit around that. When I have a 9-hour day, I consider it a very light day. In general, I refrain from planning any social activities on weeknights when I am on a project. At times you will work until midnight, and when crunch time comes you will work until 3am or even later - until the work gets done. However it's safe to say that weekends generally remain fairly sacred. The key word there is fairly. Consulting is a fast-moving, challenging industry and when the work needs to be done, it'll get done. Sometimes that will eat into your weekend. When working away from home, often you'll work at the client site until the client clocks off around 6/7pm. Then you'll go have dinner and work from your hotel room in the evening.

The pace is quick and, as a result, the lifestyle never gets cushy. But you don't join consulting for cushy.

HOW'S THE MONEY?

The money's fine. Nothing to write home about, but not much room for complaint either. You'll be earning a lot less than your friends in banking, a bit less than your friends in law, and a lot more than your friends in accounting and in industry. To be honest, as a 21-year-old it's hard to legitimately complain about starting at a salary level that already puts you in the top 5-10% of the country in terms of income. But everyone likes complaining. You can complain that bankers earn more than you, while they complain that they've not had a day off in three weeks.

IS IT FOR ME?

Is management consulting the right thing for you to be doing? That's a very important question. Unfortunately it's a question that some candidates forget to ask themselves. They hear it's prestigious, they hear it pays pretty well, and they hear buzzwords such as "challenging" and "fast-paced" and assume it'll be perfect for them. However, sometimes consulting is not what you should be doing.

It all depends on what you want from your career. Management consulting gives you a whirlwind tour of a wide range of industries and wide range of business functions, and as a result there are few jobs that match it for the flexibility it gives you later on in your career. So if you're career-agnostic, consulting is a great shout. Not only does it keep your options open, it lets you explore the jungle a little bit, and perhaps you'll find what you like. Formulating hypotheses and delivering them to the client trains you to conceptualise any commercial problem into bite-sized chunks, while being on the client site implementing a project gets you stuck into the grind. In this way, you really see what it's like on the front lines trying to attract higher revenues and keep costs down. The scenery changes quickly and you see a hell of a lot. The skills you learn are transferrable - none more so than the ability to talk to people with confidence. After a few projects conducting interviews, cold-calling customers, presenting to senior clients and defending your analysis, you quickly get comfortable with communicating with all kinds of people at all levels of seniority.

However if you want stability, then consulting is probably not for you. If you don't have high levels of energy, it'll be difficult to keep up with the travel and, more importantly, the ambiguity. I stopped bothering to plan social events on weeknights after about three weeks into the job, because they got cancelled most of the time. The constant travel can also become a drag. As glamorous as it sounds, flying from Chicago to London to Shanghai within the course of a week, seeing nothing except the insides of airports, taxis and client sites, can really take it out of you. Also, consulting doesn't pay as well as some other occupations. You're not working quite as hard as investment bankers but you're earning significantly less. And as you progress up the ladder, the difference only increases. While you'll be very comfortable, nobody gets mega-rich working in consulting. But then again, banks don't teach you how to successfully run a business on the ground. To be fair, neither does consulting, but out of any traditional career, it's the closest you'll get.

Personally I have entrepreneurial aspirations, and I can think of few jobs I could have started in that would have benefitted me more than consulting. The approach to problem-solving and the ability to prioritise tasks in a results-driven manner have been very valuable. The general business toolkit I developed enables me to have a good stab at tackling any type of problem I face in my own business, and furthermore having the background in consulting gives a hefty chunk of credibility when speaking to investors.

Overall, most people who enter consulting use it to build a great CV at the beginning of their career; few stay for the long haul. Eventually the workload, the travel, and the politics catch up. At almost every point in consulting, you can jump out into industry and earn the same amount while working fewer hours. However, your career acceleration grinds to a halt. A good rule of thumb is that a year in consulting is the equivalent of two years in industry. As a result, head-hunters will often advertise positions looking for those with 1-2 years consulting experience or 2-4 years of industry experience.

So no, it's not the dream job, but the dream job probably doesn't exist. If you're a young gun with an open mind looking to jump into the business world, there are few better places to start.

AM I RIGHT FOR IT?

So after reading all that, you still fancy a go? Yes? Genuinely? Top stuff. Part of the battle is already won. You've been told what consulting actually is, you've been told that not all the projects are for big, shiny, famous clients, you know that you'll have to give most of your life away to the job, and you're still excited. You still want that career in consulting. That's great. Now we have to talk about whether or not consulting wants you.

Consulting firms want to hire people who are good at consulting, and to become good at consulting you need certain traits. That means two things: 1. You should do whatever you can to develop these qualities, if you don't already possess them; 2. When you get interviewed, these are the qualities the interviewer is looking for - every question they ask will be testing to see how many of these qualities you possess, so you'd better be oozing with them, all the time.

Consulting firms want to hire somebody who is:

1. Passionate about business
2. Well-structured
3. Results-focused
4. An information sponge
5. Team-oriented
6. A great communicator
7. A high performer

Let's talk about each of those a little more...

1. <u>Passionate about business</u>

I won't dwell on this one as it's a no brainer. All day, every single day, you're dealing with businesses and business models. You should be thriving on it. If you're not fascinated by how businesses work, you'll quickly get bored and wish you were doing something else with your time.

2. <u>Well-structured</u>

Being well-structured is extraordinarily important in the world of management consulting. A huge part of the job is to take a complex, seemingly impenetrable problem and break it down into digestible chunks that can then be solved bit by bit. For example, if you need to build a spreadsheet to model a market, you need to be able to identify all the market drivers and how they are likely to affect the key outputs in which you're interested, including any and all weightings, multipliers and feedback loops, etc. And then you'll have to be able to tie it all together and explain the whole process to the client in a way they can easily understand. The trick is to be able to structure and explain concepts with perspicuity, without being Procrustean.

3. Results-focused

Time pressure will become part of the furniture when you're on a project. There'll be fifty things that need to be done in absolutely no time at all, and you'll need to be able to prioritise between them. There's a concept that's used widely in consulting: the 80/20 rule. Eighty percent of the value can be delivered in twenty percent of the time. You need to be able to figure out and focus on that eighty percent to enable you to move on to the next thing as quickly as you can. As well as helping you to deal with pressing deadlines, being results-focused also ensures that you never lose sight of the overall aim of the project, and always deliver what the project promised.

4. An information sponge

The ability to assimilate large volumes of information in a short space of time will make your life as a consultant easier by an order of magnitude. When researching industries and companies, you'll have to get to grips with dozens of annual reports, market intelligence reports and analyses, interview transcripts, surveys, charts, etc. in a short period of time to form a view which then serves as the foundation for advising the client. The ability to not just read the material but absorb and assimilate the information in a way that you can then distill into cogent messages is good. To do it quickly is key.

5. Team-oriented

Consultants work in case teams. At times you'll be at the client site with the same team for months, spending more than 12 hours a day together, working, eating, playing as a team. Therefore, while you need to be individually brilliant, your ability to function as a part of a team is paramount. That means not being too precious about your ideas, being able to take in other peoples' perspectives and consider them without bias, and just be pleasant to be around for such a long period of time. As you move up the ladder, then being able to utilise everyone's time efficiently when managing a team is also very important.

6. A great communicator

You might have the best analysis in the world, but if you're unable to get the message across to the rest of your team or to the client, it's not very useful. Consulting firms look for candidates who are articulate in their written and oral communication. There are few things that lose you credibility with the client more than sounding like a blubbering idiot when presenting your expertise. Your client stakeholders are usually extremely busy, so you need to give them the information they require as accurately as possible with as little fuss as possible.

7. A high performer

Whatever you do, you do it very well indeed. This comprises a whole host of lovely adjectives that combine to result in generally excellent human beings: smart, hard-working, conscientious, creative, et cetera et cetera. You get the idea. You're the type of person who can be trusted to complete a task given to them to the exacting standards that clients demand, and beyond.

If you possess the qualities laid out above, your life will be so much easier. Just act natural and make sure your personality comes across. If you recognise weaknesses, then you need to work on not only appearing to have these qualities, but how to actually hone them so you become more attractive to consulting firms. You'll also be a damn sight more successful if you get in.

There is a ton of literature online about each of the above topics/qualities and I suggest you go take a look. The next section of this book reveals which part of the application process tests for which of these qualities, and how best to get across to the firm that you not only possess them, but you have both developed and demonstrated your mastery of them in your previous life.

PART 2

BREAKING AND ENTERING

The application process for management consulting is pretty straightforward. Most firms require just a CV and Cover Letter to submit an application. The overall process looks a little like this

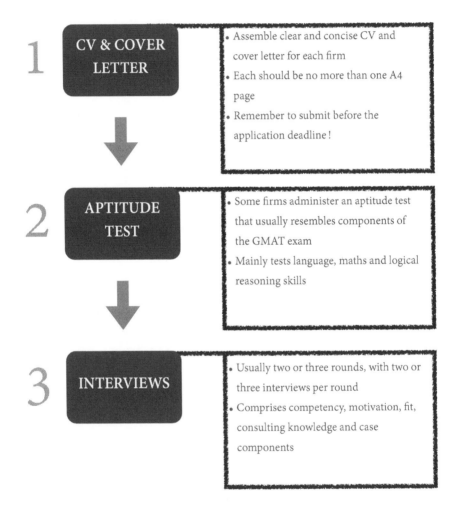

1

CV & COVER LETTER

- Assemble clear and concise CV and cover letter for each firm
- Each should be no more than one A4 page
- Remember to submit before the application deadline!

2

APTITUDE TEST

- Some firms administer an aptitude test that usually resembles components of the GMAT exam
- Mainly tests language, maths and logical reasoning skills

3

INTERVIEWS

- Usually two or three rounds, with two or three interviews per round
- Comprises competency, motivation, fit, consulting knowledge and case components

GETTING THE INTERVIEW:
CV AND COVER LETTER

INITIAL PREPARATION

The first thing you need to do is plan. Go to all the events held at your university - many have consultancy fairs where firms come to market themselves to graduates – and talk to actual consultants. Get an idea of how much they enjoy their jobs, what kind of work their office does specifically, and what advice they would have for the application process. When we meet students at careers fairs, the most annoying ones are always the ones that try to impress/suck up to you there and then. It's too obvious. Chances are we won't remember you, and even if we do we're unlikely to be a position to push your application forward. You're much better off building natural rapport, and getting great advice about the application and the interview, rather than trying to get a job off me right there.

In the process of gathering information, I'd recommend making a spreadsheet. Not only will it help you keep the entire processed organised, being able to create spreadsheets will come in very handy indeed when you're working in consulting, so if you're not already familiar, it's time to get familiar. List out every firm you intend to apply to and note down their application deadlines, potential interview dates, web addresses, HR contact details, and anything you know about the firm's application process – how many rounds of interview there are, whether or not there is a test, etc. It's also useful to put down the contact details of anyone you may have met from the company, and reach out to them for advice just before each interview. Finally make a note of the office address of each firm so you know where you're going if you get an interview.

This is also a good place to keep track of your progress with each firm, so you know what's coming up next. Simply keeping organised will ensure that you don't throw away all the hard work you put into preparing your application by missing your interview.

Finally I'd recommend setting up a Google Alert for each of the firms you're applying to. If anything about them hits the news, you'll be kept in the loop!

THE CV

A consulting firm in London will receive thousands of applications for graduate positions every year. Depending on the firm, it will be looking to recruit between 5 and 25 graduates. The majority of those culled are done so at the CV stage, and decisions are made pretty quickly. In many firms the consultants themselves filter through the CVs. This is partly because they generally know best what to look for, but also because a firm's pool of consultants represents the largest pool of manpower, which is required to get through all the applications. Many if not most of these consultants will be on consulting projects in the office, and need to get through the pile as quickly as possible so they can get back to their work and hopefully finish at a reasonable hour that evening. Therefore, the amount of attention each CV receives is, unfortunately, not as much as it perhaps deserves. If your CV hasn't impressed within the first 20 or 30 seconds, it'll get thrown in the "we regret to inform you" pile. Sounds a bit harsh, but the reality is that the sheer number of CVs that will impress in the first 20 seconds is already too high. Every year when we go through CVs in our office, we sort them into three piles: "yes", "no" and "maybe". By the end of the day, the "no" pile gets sent bad news, and the "maybe" pile also gets sent bad news because we realise that the "yes" pile is already twice the size it should be. So then we go through the "yes" pile again and get rid of half of those.

The message I'm trying to get across is that the CV stage is when the ratios are the worst. It's the hurdle where most people fall. So you need to do every within your power to ensure that your CV is the absolute best it could be, and that you've spared no effort in perfecting it.

Content

So first and foremost, we're going to assume you've got good content. A decent degree (2.1 minimum) from a top university is required – Russell Group is fine, but Oxbridge/ London certainly helps. If the university you attended wasn't particularly prestigious, that's fine. You just have to make sure that you did incredibly well on your course (first class degree) and have very solid work experience. The subject doesn't really matter as long as it's not something universally recognised as codswallop, like Geography or Land Economy. Something quantitative such as Engineering or Economics will help you a little depending on which firm you're applying to, but given that you're probably already doing/have already done your degree, there's little we can do about it now. We're going to assume you have decent work experience (at least one relevant internship/entrepreneurial experience lasting more than 4 weeks) and extra-curricular achievements (sports team captain, charity work, musical achievement, etc)*. Spend a little time collating everything you've done that could go in your CV – every leadership position you've had, every piece of work experience, and anything else significant. That doesn't include prizes you won in primary school, or the time you came top 5% nationally in your Maths GCSE. Any prizes or extra-curricular achievements you had prior to starting your undergraduate course are irrelevant, unless you won the Nobel Prize when you were 15, or something really impressive like that (but if that were the case then you should try to do something more awesome than consulting, perhaps!) Organise each of these things under the titles "Education", "Work Experience", and "Positions of Responsibility", and note down some details for each one – what you did and what you concretely achieved. It's very important that you know very clearly what it is your responsibilities were, and what was directly achieved due to your involvement. Not only will you be able to show that you are a genuine high performer who can lead teams and get things done, you also show that you are results oriented by dispatching with the waffle.

Then, you need to think very hard about which experiences and achievements are the most relevant to consulting and paint you as the character most suitable and most likely to succeed in a fast-paced, team-oriented business environment. These are the ones that you can use to articulate your finest qualities. Prioritise the experiences that have given you experience of business – these will be the points that differentiate you from all the rugby team captains and academic prize-winners. Remember the seven qualities you just read about in the previous section? Those are the qualities you want to be getting across. Delete everything else. What you have left will constitute around 95% of your CV.

The remaining 5% is admin: name, contact details, date of birth, nationality, etc. There is no need to put a reference unless specifically requested by the firm to which you're applying.

Structure and formatting

Your CV should fit comfortably on one side of A4. If it's longer than that, you're either trying to fit in too much information, or you can try to play around with spacings/formatting in your word processor software. Remember we're trying to be both clear and concise. Not only does keeping the CV short help the guy who has to look at it get through it quicker, it also means you don't dilute your most impressive positions and achievements with those that were perhaps less so.

Your CV also needs to be very easy to follow – it ought to flow well. You essentially want to have a list of experiences and achievements organised by category (Education, Work Experience, Positions of Responsibility) and in chronological order. For each experience you then need two or three bullet points detailing exactly what your responsibilities were and what you achieved. If there's space at the end, then put in a few points showing what a lovely well-rounded individual you are. The key principle to remember when structuring your CV is consistency. Make sure the date is always in the same position and format, your bullet points are aligned and your titles are the same size, etc.

Ensure that all the information is presented appropriately. Your name should obviously be in a prominent position, and the content should be structured such that if the

---

* If you don't have any those things, it's going to be tough to get through the CV stage. Depending on how close you are to the deadline, consider delaying your application by a year and going out there and getting the relevant experience.

reader can only spend five seconds looking at your CV, they will get the most relevant information immediately from the titles. Then, if more time is available, the information is presented such that it is very easy for the reader to delve into.

In terms of formatting, keep it conservative. Management consulting is a very professional industry, so your CV must exude professionalism. You can't get an interview by trying to stand out with the formatting, but you can certainly lose one. That means no fancy icons, no snazzy colours and no crazy fonts. Use formatting only to distinguish between different text levels in the document, in order to present a well-ordered and logical structure that guides the reader through your experiences and achievements.

Ultimately, your CV is the only representation you have in the firm before you go for interview. Make sure you're happy with that representation.

On the next page you'll find an example of the kind of structure you want your CV to follow.

Tel (Mob): 07123456789, Email: john@smith.com Address: 94 Piccadilly, London, UK, W1J 7BP

JOHN SMITH

NATIONALITY: BRITISH   D.O.B.: 17/04/1992

EDUCATION

2010 – 2013   **UNIVERSITY OF ANYTHING, COUNTRY**

- BA Degree Subject, Second Class Division One

2003 – 2010   **HIGH SCHOOL, TOWN, COUNTRY**

- 4 A-Levels - all at grade A (Subject 1, Subject 2, Subject 3, Subject 4)
- 12 GCSEs – all at grade A*

WORK EXPERIENCE

2012 – 2013   **COMPANY 1 – TEAM – POSITION**

- Description of the company, the team you were in and the responsibilities you held
- Description of what you achieved in this position and hard skills learnt

2011 – 2012   **COMPANY 2 – TEAM – POSITION**

- Description of the company, the team you were in and the responsibilities you held
- Description of what you achieved in this position and hard skills learnt

2010 – 2011   **COMPANY 3 – TEAM – POSITION**

- Description of the company, the team you were in and the responsibilities you held
- Description of what you achieved in this position and hard skills learnt

POSITIONS OF RESPONSIBILITY

2012 – 2013   **ORGANISATION 1 - POSITION**

- Description of the organisation, the team you were in and the responsibilities you held
- Description of what you achieved in this position and hard skills learnt

2011 – 2012   **ORGANISATION 2 - POSITION**

- Description of the organisation, the team you were in and the responsibilities you held
- Description of what you achieved in this position and hard skills learnt

2010 – 2011   **ORGANISATION 3 - POSITION**

- Description of the organisation, the team you were in and the responsibilities you held
- Description of what you achieved in this position and hard skills learnt

SKILLS, INTERESTS AND OTHER ACTIVITIES

LANGUAGES Language 1: Proficiency Level; Language 2: Proficiency Level
SPORT Sports teams you have represented
MUSIC Any musical interests or certifications you may have
OTHER Other information, such as volunteering work or traveling experiences

MOST COMMON CV MISTAKE

I'll be honest – there's not a lot you can do if your credentials don't fit. There are already far too many people with the right educational background and relevant work experience. Apart from actual lack of experience, the most common mistake I've seen in applicants' CVs is including too much irrelevant information. Some people put in random summer jobs, while others explain their love of pottery in far too much detail, or put down every single one of their GCSE grades. Don't do that. A less obvious mistake is including information about projects or jobs that were incredibly important in context, but do not bring any value to consulting. For example, Engineering is a strong degree from which to apply to consulting. However when talking about their final year project, many candidates feel the urge to include all the technical details that mean nothing to anyone who didn't study Engineering. Details that, no doubt, were incredibly impressive in the technical context of the project, sadly have no relevance to consulting or the business world. And the kicker is that by including that information, you're not only adding little value to your application, you're also using up the space that could be filled with something more relevant. Instead of technical details, you should be sharing the skills you learnt, and articulating the fact that you are a creative problem-solver who works incredibly hard to overcome challenges. Including information that doesn't get these points across is a waste of valuable space on your CV. Make sure every single sentence on your CV has a reason for being there.

THE COVER LETTER

While having a single CV for all your consulting applications is pretty much fine, having a single cover letter is not. For one thing, the name of the firm you're applying to is on that letter. Every year at my firm we'll see a few that slip through the net with the name of a competitor in the cover letter. Everyone has a good chuckle and the application goes in the bin. This isn't because we found out you're applying to somewhere else. Anyone that wants to get into consulting will be applying to many firms - it's the sensible thing to do. The reason the application goes in the bin is that the mistake indicates the applicant lacks attention to detail, or that they simply do not see their application as important enough to proof read their cover letter. Neither of these traits is desirable. Same goes for typos.

Furthermore, each cover letter needs to be different because each firms sees itself differently. They each have their own histories and values that inform the kind of person they want to hire. That doesn't mean a template letter with "find/replace" on the firm name and core values. What it means is that the information you include, the key experiences and skills you highlight must be tailored to the firm to which the application is to be sent. The content of your cover letter must be directly relevant to what the firm is looking for in a candidate. The added benefit of doing your homework on exactly what each firm wants is that you'll know exactly what each firm wants! This will help you out in the interview, but more importantly it'll help you to figure out if you'll enjoy working for that firm. Far too many candidates will try to fit themselves to the mould that firms want to hire. You ought to take a step back and think to yourself – is this what I really want to be? If not, then you'd probably be better served looking elsewhere. What you don't want is to go through the entire process and start working in a consultancy, only to realise that you hate being the kind of person you need to be to succeed there.

So how do you make your cover letter stand out? First and foremost, you have to start strong. Just as with CVs, each cover letter gets very little time unless it grabs the reader's attention. You'll probably get ten or fifteen seconds to show that you're different to other candidates. So instead of the bog-standard "I did this, then I did this, then I did this", put down something that actually adds value. Something more along the lines of "I achieved X, which trained me in quality Y, which is a rare trait and matters in consulting because of Z". Just like your CV, your cover letter should be no longer than a page of A4, and if the page looks too full then you've written too much. So in the limited amount of space you have, you must differentiate yourself from other candidates. To be perfectly honest, this isn't that difficult because hardly anyone puts in the effort to make their cover letter stand out. Most are just find/replace jobs. So your first paragraph should carry your knockout points – What are the top two reasons you are different to the other thousand excellent candidates? Why are you more suitable for the role at this particular firm than 95% of the applications they receive? If you have a killer CV, then you can probably get away with a bog standard cover letter. However a great cover letter can get an average-looking CV through to the interview stage.

Your cover letter should certainly not be just a repeat of your CV in prose. Talk about the things that you can't put on a CV. Talk about the passion you have had for business since you were young. Let the reader know that you've done your research – really done your research – on the firm, its projects, practices, and culture. Perhaps explain your view on a market that the firm focuses on, or give an example of research/projects that you have undertaken that are similar to what the firm takes on, and explain your competence and enthusiasm to engage in more of that kind of work. Describe the experiences you've had that have led you to share the same core values as your prospective employer. Firms want to hire sincere candidates, and can see through the ones that just went on the website to copy and paste the list of corporate values. I'd suggest you list them down in your first draft so that you can elaborate on them after you've got the rest of the structure down.

What will be especially impressive is if you can talk about the specific type of work that a consultant would undertake and then explain that you already have experience in the field: e.g. competency in building market models, assessing competitive landscapes, conducting research and interviews, synthesising arguments and creating hypotheses from available data will all put you at an advantage compared to other candidates, as it means that there will be a smaller gap to fill between the level you start at and the level at which you need to be in order to start functioning as a useful consultant.

This final point should be obvious: your cover letter is the first opportunity you have to show your abilities in written communication, so you must ensure a high level of professionalism. No abbreviations, no contractions, no colloquialisms. While remaining professional, your letter needs to ooze enthusiasm and dedication to the career.

On the next pages you'll find an example CV and Cover Letter. Remember they are merely examples. Feel free to play around! (In the CV I have unfortunately had to sacrifice content quantity in the interest of keeping the font large enough to read, but you get the idea!)

JOHN SMITH

NATIONALITY: BRITISH   D.O.B.: 17/04/1992

EDUCATION

2010 – 2013   **UNIVERSITY OF OXFORD, UK**
- BA History and Economics, First Class

2003 – 2010   **HIGH SCHOOL, TOWN, UK**
- 4 A-Levels - all at grade A* (Mathematics, English, Economics, History)
- 12 GCSEs – all at grade A*

WORK EXPERIENCE

2012 – 2013   **THE MCBAIN CONSULTING GROUP – INTERNSHIP**
- 12-week internship, working on an automotive marketing project, conducted market research as well as quantitative and qualitative analysis
- Supported the successful completion of a project that increased the client's marketing efficiency in every channel by an average of 24%; Gained significant client exposure and market research skills

2011 – 2012   **SILVERMAN SACHS – INVESTMENT BANKING DIVISION – INTERNSHIP**
- 8-week programme supporting transactions in the Mining & Metals team
- Built DCF models to analyse three potential investments, one of which supported a live transaction that eventually came to fruition for a consideration of over GBP 300m

POSITIONS OF RESPONSIBILITY

2012 – 2013   **UNIVERSITY FINANCE SOCIETY - PRESIDENT**
- Led a committee of eight members to run the Finance Society, whose membership exceeded 1,000 students
- Organised the annual conference attended by more than 800 participants, as well as overseeing the day-to-day running of the society and arranging multiple speaker and career guidance events

2010 – 2011   **UNIVERSITY HELP THE HOMELESS – SPONSORSHIP OFFICER**
- Responsible for securing sponsorship in Help The Homeless, a university organisation that aims to improve the lives of homeless individuals in the local area
- Led a team of four volunteers to secure funding of over GBP 2,000 in seven months, which was an all-time record for the organisation

SKILLS, INTERESTS AND OTHER ACTIVITIES

LANGUAGES	French: Fluent; Spanish: Fluent; Arabic: Intermediate
SPORT	Represented Oxford University Basketball team from 2011 to 2013
MUSIC	ABRSM Grade 8 Piano and Violin
OTHER	Cycled solo from John O'Groats to Casablanca in 2012

John Smith
94 Piccadilly
London
S1J 7BP
United Kingdom
28th November
2013

Consulting Firm Ltd
56 St James' Place
London
SW1Y 6RH

Dear Sir/Madam,

It gives me much pleasure to submit to you my application for the entry level Consultant position you offer. I am confident that the unique combination of my rigorous education, existing financial and analytical skills, dedication to work and structured mind place me in good stead to thrive in Consulting Firm.

Strategy consulting appeals to me threefold. Firstly, I am excited by the notion of delving into the intricacies of organisations ranging in both industry and business practice. I also recognise that as a result of the wide variety of circumstances strategy consultants are exposed to, the industry provides an excellent opportunity to learn how to make businesses successful. Thirdly, I relish the challenge, both intellectual and practical, that strategy consulting presents.

As a final year student in History and Economics from the University of Oxford, I am firstly accustomed to producing high quality work to strict deadlines in a pressured environment. The course itself, combining the quantitative analysis of economics with the more qualitative assessment required in History, has allowed me to develop my skills of analytical problem solving, efficient assimilation of information and communicating complex ideas with clarity. Meanwhile, having worked assiduously in various extra-curricular roles and work environments, I have both developed and demonstrated my abilities in teamwork, oral communication and leadership. Through chairing meetings, preparing presentations and presenting funding proposals to potential sponsors, I have discovered a passion for solving problems and delivering results – a rare quality that I believe would serve well at Consulting Firm.

I very much appreciate your time and consideration, and would welcome an opportunity to discuss my application in more detail. I look forward to hearing from you.

Yours sincerely,

John Smith

GETTING THE INTERVIEW: APTITUDE TEST

Many firms administer an aptitude test before offering any interviews. More often than not, this will comprise one or many components of a GMAT style test, with verbal, reasoning and quantitative elements. In addition, firms sometimes include questions that assess a candidate's ability to analyse data and reach conclusions in commercial scenarios in a short amount of time. The test is not designed to check on any specific knowledge. Instead, it's to discover if you possess the qualities laid out in the first section: whether or not you'd make a good consultant. It will test your ability to quickly calculate numbers, your business sense, your ability to assimilate information quickly and your ability to quickly assess and analyse information presented to you.

The absolute key to nailing this style of test is practice, practice and practice! No amount of advice I can give you will be as good as doing so many questions your head hurts, and then doing some more. In the following pages, I present the different types of questions you will receive during the test, along with some sample questions to give you an idea of what they look like. An online search will yield a multitude of websites that offer an almost endless supply of sample questions for you to practise on. I highly recommend you do this. One thing to bear in mind is that when you sit the test, it will be extremely time-pressured. So make sure you learn to get these questions done quickly.

VERBAL & COMPREHENSION

This is to test your ability to take in and understand written information. Most of the time, this will be presented to you as either a reading comprehension task, or a summary task. In the former, you will be asked to read a passage and then answer a number of questions on the content of the passage. In the latter, you will be asked to summarise a passage of text, with a specific word limit designed to force you to think about the key message of the original article. In a comprehension task your objective is to "get the message" that's being presented to you. In a summary task you'll, in addition, be required to "play back" what you read, picking out the key points that are the most important.

There's a whole host of information online about how to excel at summary tasks that will do a much better job than I can in a small section of this book. However, you can find some example reading comprehension questions below. Answers to all questions are provided at the end of the section.

Read the following passage:

The chieftain of a small primitive tribe is as a rule in a position to concentrate in his hands all legislative, administrative, and judiciary power. His will is the law. He is both executive and judge.

But it is different when the despot has succeeded in expanding the size of his realm. As he lacks ubiquity, he must delegate a part of his power to subordinates. They are, in their districts, his deputies, acting in his name and under his auspices. In fact they become local despots only nominally subject to the mighty overlord who has appointed them. They rule their provinces according to their own will; they become satraps. The great king has the power to discharge them and to appoint a successor. But that is no remedy either. The new governor also soon becomes an almost independent satrap. What some critics—wrongly—assert with regard to representative democracy, namely, that the people is sovereign only on election day, is literally true with regard to such a system of despotism; the king is sovereign in the provinces only on the day he appoints a new governor.

In what does the position of such a provincial governor differ from that of the manager of a business branch? The manager of the whole concern hands over an aggregate to the newly appointed branch manager and gives him one directive only: Make profits. This order, the observance of which is continuously checked by the accounts, is sufficient to make the branch a subservient part of the whole concern and to give to its manager's action the direction aimed at by the central manager. But if the despot, for whom his own arbitrary decision is the only principle of government, appoints a governor and says to him: "Be my deputy in this province," he makes the deputy's arbitrariness supreme in this province. He renounces, at least temporarily, his own power to the benefit of the governor.

In order to avoid this outcome the king tries to limit the governor's powers by issuing directives and instructions. Codes, decrees, and statutes tell the governors of the provinces and their subordinates what to do if such and such a problem arises. Their free discretion is now limited; their first duty is now to comply with the regulations. It is true that their arbitrariness is now restricted in so far as the regulations must be applied. But at the same time the whole character of their management changes. They are no longer eager to deal with each case to the best of their abilities; they are no longer anxious to find the most appropriate solution for every problem. Their main concern is to comply with the rules and regulations, no matter whether they are reasonable or contrary to what was intended. The first virtue of an administrator is to abide by the codes and decrees. He becomes a bureaucrat.

- from *Bureaucracy* by Ludwig von Mises (1962)

Question 1: What is the main topic of the passage?

    A. The method by which a chieftain of a small tribe rules his subjects

    B. How a business can make more profits by expanding into new areas

    C. How red tape develops in expanding organisations

    D. Power struggles between a king and his governor

    E. A comparison between representative democracy and despotism

Question 2: The author believes bureaucracy is created when:

    A. Power is delegated from a superior to a subordinate

    B. Arbitrary decision is the only principle of government within an organisation

    C. A newly appointed business branch manager is instructed to make profits

    D. New problems arise in a province where a governor has not been given specific instructions on how to deal with them

    E. A despot, fearing loss of power, places limitations on a governor's discretion

Question 3: What does the author imply with the sentence "*The first virtue of an administrator is to abide by the codes and decrees*"?

    A. That all administrators are very skillful in abiding by codes and decrees that are issued by the king

    B. Historically, it was considered virtuous for administrators to abide by all the codes and decrees passed down by the despot

    C. As a result of having to obey decrees and statutes, the administrator is distracted from effective governance

    D. Abiding by the rules is a skill that administrators must learn before all others

    E. The main strength of administrators is that they abide by codes and decrees issued by a despot

Read the following passage:

It is significant that one of the commonest objections to competition is that it is "blind." It is not irrelevant to recall that to the ancients blindness was an attribute of their deity of justice. Although competition and justice may have little else in common, it is as much a commendation of competition as of justice that it is no respecter of persons.

That it is impossible to foretell who will be the lucky ones or whom disaster will strike, that rewards and penalties are not shared out according to somebody's views about the merits or demerits of different people but depend on their capacity and their luck, is as important as that, in framing legal rules, we should not be able to predict which particular person will gain and which will lose by their application.

And this is nonetheless true, because in competition chance and good luck are often as important as skill and foresight in determining the fate of different people. The choice open to us is not between a system in which everybody will get what he deserves according to some absolute and universal standard of right, and one where the individual shares are determined partly by accident or good or ill chance, but between a system where it is the will of a few persons that decides who is to get what, and one where it depends at least partly on the ability and enterprise of the people concerned and partly on unforeseeable circumstances.

This is no less relevant because in a system of free enterprise chances are not equal, since such a system is necessarily based on private property and (though perhaps not with the same necessity) on inheritance, with the differences in opportunity which these create. There is, indeed, a strong case for reducing this inequality of opportunity as far as congenital differences permit and as it is possible to do so without destroying the impersonal character of the process by which everybody has to take his chance and no person's view about what is right and desirable overrules that of others.

The fact that the opportunities open to the poor in a competitive society are much more restricted than those open to the rich does not make it less true that in such a society the poor are much more free than a person commanding much greater material comfort in a different type of society.

Although under competition the probability that a man who starts poor will reach great wealth is much smaller than is true of the man who has inherited property, it is not only possible for the former, but the competitive system is the only one where it depends solely on him and not on the favors of the mighty, and where nobody can prevent a man from attempting to achieve this result.

- from *The Road to Serfdom* by F.A. Hayek (1944)

Question 4: From the passage, it can be inferred that the author would agree with all the following **except**:

    A. A freely competitive society, despite its shortcomings, is preferable to the alternative

    B. Society should be able to pass laws in order to punish those whom it deems to be immoral

    C. It is important in society that a person's wealth should depend, at least partly, on their own ability and enterprise

    D. We should try to ensure that people are born with as equal an opportunity as possible to succeed in life

    E. To criticise free competition for being "blind" is a fallacy, as its blindness is one of its virtues

Question 5: The passage is most probably intended to:

    A. Make people aware of the virtues of free competition in society

    B. Argue the case for increasing inheritance tax

    C. Make people recognise that there are fewer opportunities open to the poor than to the rich in a freely competitive society

    D. Serve as the introduction for a more detailed discussion on justice

    E. Analyse the possible repercussions of "blind" competition

REASONING QUESTIONS

Reasoning tests assess your logic skills, testing your ability to recognise patterns and analyse simple, conceptual problems. They often consist of number series, ciphers and logical problems. Being able to solve these problems quickly and accurately can give a very important advantage when consulting: you are more likely to be able to diagnose commercial problems quickly and accurately, as well as check the veracity of that diagnosis with greater speed and precision. Some example questions are below.

Question 1: Fred is taller than Joe, and Andrew is shorter than Fred. Who is taller between Joe and Andrew?

    A. Joe
    B. Andrew
    C. They are the same height
    D. Uncertain

Question 2: Complete the sentence: table is to wood as tyre is to...?

    A. Car
    B. Driver
    C. Wheel
    D. Rubber
    E. Metal

Question 3: Fill in the missing entry: ATL, CSO, ERR, [???]

    A. GQU
    B. KCN
    C. GIK
    D. PKQ
    E. NNK

Question 4: What number comes next in the following sequence: 6, 11, 21, 41, 81, ?

    A. 101

    B. 121

    C. 141

    D. 161

    E. 181

Question 5: "*Klickputz*" means "Fireman"; "*Magdenamen*" means "Drawbridge"; "*Cuoforc*" means "Dumptruck". Which of the following could mean "Wildfire"?

    A. Forcklick

    B. Muoklick

    C. Klicknamen

    D. Magdeporc

DATA SUFFICIENCY QUESTIONS

Data sufficiency questions test your ability to quickly gauge what conclusions you can derive from information that is presented to you. They consist of a question followed by two statements, and you must decide whether the information in the statements is sufficient to answer to question. You're not required to actually answer the question: the point is purely to work out if you have enough information to do so. A number of sample questions are below. For each question, choose from the following options:

A. Statement 1 alone is sufficient, but statement 2 alone is not sufficient to answer the question
B. Statement 2 alone is sufficient, but statement 1 alone is not sufficient to answer the question
C. Both statements taken together are sufficient to answer the question, but neither statement alone is sufficient
D. Each statement alone is sufficient to answer the question
E. Statements 1 and 2 together are not sufficient, and additional data is needed to answer the question

Question 1: How many boys in a class are over the age of 10?
1. There are 15 boys in the class
2. 35% of the class is over the age of 10

Question 2: If the buyer's premium on a painting was 25% of the final auction price, what was the final auction price?
1. The final auction price of the painting plus the buyer's premium was £12,000
2. The final auction price of the painting was 6% higher than the second highest bid

Question 3: Peter was born on January 5th. In what year was he born?

1. Peter's daughter shares his birthday and will be half his age in 2016
2. Peter's daughter will be 23 years old in 2014

Question 4: What is the value of p?

1. $2p + q = 14$
2. $p - q = 4pq - 22$

Question 5: There are four towns that lie on a single road. How far away is town D from town A?

1. Town A is 5 miles from Town C
2. The distance between Town C and Town D is twice the distance between Town A and Town B

QUANTITATIVE QUESTIONS

Consulting isn't as quant-heavy as banking is, but you'll definitely have to know your way around numbers. If nothing else, it means that you can quickly work out EBIT margins, growth rates, market shares etc. that could give you a first indication of the situation a company or market is in, which will then enable you to pick the areas on which to focus further investigation without having to waste too much time in trying to work out what's going on. The quantitative questions will generally involve quick-fire mental maths, such as the questions below. No calculators allowed!

Question 1: Which number is closest to 1/6?
A. 0.25
B. 1/3
C. 1/10
D. 0.2
E. 0.14

Question 2: Which of the following could be lengths of the sides of a right-angled triangle?
A. 2, 2, 6
B. 5, 12, 13
C. 6, 8, 14
D. 5, 10, 20
E. 4, 6, 7

Question 3: If m and n are integers, and $4m + 3n = 35$, which of the following could be the value of m?
A. 0
B. 1

C. 2

D. 3

E. 4

Question 4: In a class of 30 students, 17 study Maths and 19 study Physics. 2 study neither Maths nor Physics. How many study both?

A. 5

B. 8

C. 11

D. 13

E. 15

Question 5: What is the average of three tenths and six thousandths?

A. 153.2

B. 15.32

C. 1.532

D. 0.153

E. 0.015

INTEGRATED COMMERCIAL REASONING

Here's where all of the above come together. Questions on integrated commercial reasoning will be by far the most interesting questions you'll get, and the closest to the type of problems you'll actually need to solve on a consulting project. Most firms don't have an integrated commercial reasoning section, but some of the most prestigious will do. You'll be presented with data and asked to interpret and analyse it in the context of a business. You'll have to think logically in order to come up with sensible conclusions and recommendations. Essentially, you'll be using all the skills you need for the other sections plus a bit of business sense in order to prove that you're able to actually use your skills practically when looking at applied problems rather than purely theoretical ones. Examples overleaf.

Company X sells widgets. It made £273 million in revenue in 2013, and its revenue projections under various scenarios are presented in the following graph:

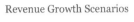

Revenue Growth Scenarios

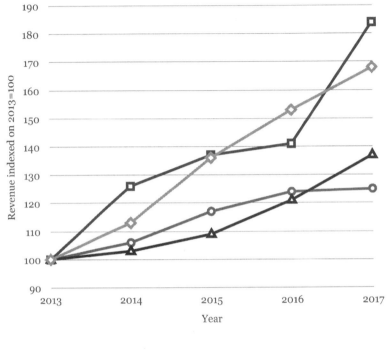

Scenario 1　　Scenario 2　　Scenario 3　　Scenario 4

Question 1: What is the best estimate for the Compound Annual Growth Rate of revenues under Scenario 3?

    A. 8%

    B. 5%

    C. 13%

    D. 23%

    E. 27%

Question 2: What is the best estimate for the extra revenue Company X would make in 2017 if Scenario 1 occurred compared to Scenario 4?

    A. £44 million

    B. £92 million

    C. £117 million

    D. £145 million

    E. £182 million

Company Y produces Lekkos, Dekkos and Frekkos. The cost structure for each of these products is shown in the graph below:

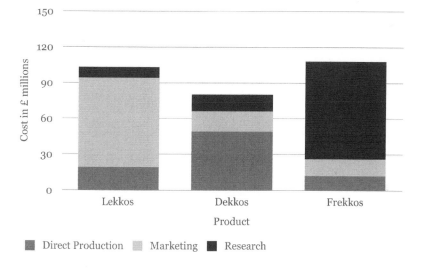

Question 3: Which of the following products are Dekkos most likely to be?

    A. Pharmaceuticals

    B. Carbonated Energy Drinks

    C. Sportswear

    D. Computer Software

E.   Microwave ovens

Question 4: If the quantity produced of all three products was cut by 50%, what is the best estimate for the total cost of all three products?

A.   £50 million

B.   £100 million

C.   £150 million

D.   £250 million

E.   £400 million

Some revenue details for Company Y are shown below:

	2013 REVENUE	AVERAGE ANNUAL REVENUE GROWTH RATE FROM 2009 TO 2013
LEKKOS	£166 million	12%
DEKKOS	£99 million	2%
FREKKOS	£180 million	8%

Question 5: Which product made the least amount of revenue in 2010?

A.   Lekkos

B.   Dekkos

C.   Frekkos

D.   There is not enough information to tell

ANSWERS TO EXAMPLE QUESTIONS

	Q1	Q2	Q3	Q4	Q5
VERBAL AND COMPREHENSION	C	E	C	B	A
REASONING QUESTIONS	D	D	A	D	B
DATA SUFFICIENCY QUESTIONS	E	A	C	C	E
QUANTITATIVE QUESTIONS	E	B	C	B	D
INTEGRATED COMMERCIAL REASONING	A	C	E	D	A

ACING THE INTERVIEW:
BEFORE THE CASE

You've secured a handful of interviews. Well done. Now here comes the really tough bit - converting that into an actual offer. Think back to the last time you aced an exam. Like, really aced it. Like, came top of the class or something. The one where you made sure you knew the syllabus inside out, you looked at all the past years' papers and tried to work out all the questions that might come up, and then meticulously went through your notes and textbooks, making more notes and distilling those notes onto index cards you could use for revising. And then you went through and did all the past years' papers to see how you did and re-revising the bits you didn't do so well in. That's the same mentality you need when preparing for a consulting interview to give yourself the best chance of acing it*.

You need to know the topic inside out, you need to know what questions might come up, and you need to rehearse the nuts off them. But this isn't just an exam; this is an exam with a twist. Two, actually:

- Delivery matters. How you come across is incredibly important. There's not a lot to say on this except that you need to remain confident (but not arrogant), calm and pleasant throughout. Being charming is a bonus. You need to be a guy/girl who the interviewer can see herself working on a project in the middle of nowhere with without wanting to punch your lights out.

---

*If you can't remember ever doing this, you're either incredibly smart, or incredibly lucky to get an interview; try to imagine what those poor sods that had to actually study were going through.

- You're not looking to get the right answers. Your answers need to more right than all the other candidates. And if they've prepared, they'll probably have all the right answers. So on top of being right, you need to shine.

This section of the book tells you what you can expect from the interview, what you need to be prepared for and how best to prepare. Keep in mind as you prepare, and especially as you walk into the interview, that every single part of it is used to assess your suitability as a consultant. The way you answer even trivial-seeming questions has an impact on how you're perceived. However, don't let this make you too nervous. Don't forget to remain natural and pleasant. After all, firms want to hire a lovely human being.

Ninety-nine percent of interviews will have the same kind of content, although the order might change. You will be asked questions about yourself and your experience, you'll be tested on your general business awareness, you'll be asked about your motivations for consulting and for the firm, and you'll be given a case interview or two. Finally you'll also have a chance to ask questions to your interviewer. This section talks about all of these questions. For each type of question I present a number of examples. These are by no means exhaustive, but I recommend you prepare answers to *all of them.* That means writing down and remembering your answers to every single example question. If you do that, then even if a different question comes up, it certainly won't take you by surprise, because it will just be a different take on one of the questions you've prepared for.

What I can't do is give you the specific answer to every single potential question that might come up. That's not possible, and not the point. What this section does is prepare you for what kind of questions are likely to come up, why they're being asked, and how to approach answering them.

A BRIEF NOTE ON CONFIDENCE

The impression you want to give in your interview is one of confidence, competence and enthusiasm. The trouble is that job interviews can be bloody scary. And scary doesn't generally inspire confidence. It tends to do the opposite. So what can be done? The answer is to strike a pose. Before you go into your interview, go somewhere isolated, such as a bathroom cubicle, and strike a power pose for a full minute. Imagine you've just won the 100m sprint at the Olympics – strike the pose you would strike for the cameras. Arms out-stretched, chest out – full on champion.

I know it sounds absurd. Actually, it sounds completely ridiculous. If you're a normal human being, you'll feel incredibly silly doing it. But *do it*. Not because it's what they do in the movies, but because there's peer-reviewed science to back it up. In 2010, researchers at Columbia Graduate School of Business ran a study that showed that certain postures cause statistically significant neuroendocrine and behavioural changes for both male and female participants. High power postures where your arms are out and your chest is out resulted in higher levels of testosterone and lower levels of cortisol in your system, which leads to increased feeling of power and confidence. (If you don't believe me, look up *Carney, Cuddy & Yap, 2010 – Power Posing: Brief Nonverbal Displays affect Neuroendocrine Levels and Risk Tolerance*). The implication is that just by strike a powerful pose for one full minute, you are psychologically and physiologically affected, causing you to become more confident.

This also applies in the interview itself – don't shrink into your seat, as your confidence will drain away. (The posture thing works the other way round too). They key isn't to look intimidating, rather it's to adopt a posture that will bring out your confident side and set you at ease.

CV SUMMARY

Perhaps the most common way to start an interview is with the CV summary. This serves a number of purposes for the interviewer: to get the low-down on you if they've not had time to look at your CV properly, to gauge your ability to present information with which you're familiar, to see how familiar you really are with your own CV, and to see how you are at structuring information. This is an immediate area in which you can differentiate yourself.

The CV summary could be thrown at you in a number of different ways, and the first step is to recognise it for what it is. The interviewer could approach it directly ("Please give me a run-through of your CV"), or they could be quite subtle about it ("Tell me about yourself", "What's your background?", etc).

However it's introduced, the two key things to keep in mind when running through your CV are to be structured and deliver with confidence. This matters even more than the content. Of course I'm not saying that what you say doesn't matter – you still need to illustrate why your experience and education make you the perfect person for the job. However, by the time you get to the interview stage, you can be pretty sure that your CV is good enough. That's why they gave you an interview. But you can also be sure that all the other interviewees also have great CVs. So you've got to differentiate yourself. The value-add is in your delivery of the CV summary, not the CV itself. By being structured in your delivery of the CV summary, you'll not only very clearly deliver the content, you'll also immediately show the interviewer that you are able to concisely synthesise the main points of a document, drawing out the most important things they ought to know. Furthermore, a confident delivery immediately shows the interviewer that you would be very comfortable in a client-facing role.

Your CV summary should take you less than 60 seconds to deliver without feeling particularly rushed. This goes by very quickly. The key is to be selective about the information you give. If you've followed the advice given earlier on, your CV will already be fairly concise. Unless there is something very impressive that precedes it (VERY impressive), start with your undergraduate education. What grades you achieved or prizes you won in high school, any summer jobs you had, or that band you were in as a teenager are irrelevant. The overall structure for a CV summary should be something like this:

I.   **Undergraduate (and postgraduate) education:**
    A.   Course and institution

II. **Experience # 1**
    A.   Responsibilities and achievements
    B.   Key personal outcomes

III. **Experience # 2**
    A.   Responsibilities and achievements
    B.   Key personal outcomes

IV. **Experience # 3**
    A.   Responsibilities and achievements
    B.   Key personal outcomes

V.   **Next steps - Why consulting? Why this firm?**

Chances are you will not have enough time to expand too much on any of these points, which is fine, because that's what the next part of the interview is for. For now, just give a one liner to get across the main messages – this is what I was responsible for, these are the results I achieved, and here's how I developed as a person. You might not even have time to get three points of experience in, or you might throw in an extra one. Whatever. That's fine. Just make sure you choose the experiences that have been most rewarding and substantive for you. A bit of variety also helps. If you were finance officer at three different societies, it doesn't make sense to talk about all of them, unless they were substantially different roles and presented different challenges. After you've been through once how you learnt to manage incomings and out-goings for an organisation and had to fundraise and pitch to sponsors, talking about how you did the same thing somewhere else will only waste the valuable time that you could be spending talking about your experiences optimising processes at a small start-up you helped out with, or whatever other exciting things you've done.

So start with your undergraduate education and proceed chronologically. Give the role and organisation of each piece of experience, briefly describe your responsibilities and achievements, and finish by telling the interviewer how you developed as a result of it. Then move on to the next one. Remember, they should be one-liners only.

Be specific with your responsibilities and be very specific with your achievements. Nebulous terms like "I was responsible for strategy", or "I drastically improved the organisation" are fairly meaningless and add very little value to your case. Instead, give examples that are quantifiable and palpable. Saying things like "I chaired weekly meetings of the 4-man executive committee to discuss overall strategic direction", "I devised a marketing plan that increased event participation by 40%" not only give the interviewer a clearer sense of what you actually did, they show that you are results-oriented. Being vague will at best not differentiate you from other candidates, and at worst can give the interviewer the impression that you are trying to hide how passive your role was.

Key personal outcomes are the skills or insights you gained from the experience that have made experience worth putting on your CV - the very same skills and insights that make you a more attractive candidate to the firm. Perhaps your role as society president gave you experience of leading a diverse team of rivals, or maybe your time spent pitching for sponsorship gave you the ability to speak to and persuade senior stakeholders with confidence and clarity. If you had a formal internship, talk about the hard skills you learnt during that time. In any case, each one of your experiences needs to have a "so what?" to go with it.

So sit down with a printed copy of your CV and pick out the really crucial points of experience on there. Write them down in list format and then then memorise a short, snappy description for each one. It's even better if your experiences are linked in some way. Did one experience lead you to wanting to try out another? Explaining that your selection of experiences has been deliberate shows that you are conscientious when it comes to your career. Finally, talk about your next steps. Talk about the fact that you're trying to break into management consulting. Obviously you are. The interviewer knows you are. You're sat in the damn interview. But you say it to show that it's a deliberate, considered choice, and you're not just doing it because all your friends are/you think it pays well/it's one of a bunch of careers you're trying your luck in. And for heaven's sake talk about why. If you can give your reasons for wanting to join consulting, it can show you're actually motivated by the industry, and if nothing else saves the interviewer from having to ask you the question later on. Remember - it's all about differentiating yourself, and confidently articulating your reasons for wanting to join the industry without being prompted is an easy win.

So draft out your CV summary and practise it in front on the mirror until you can memorise it. Not word-for-word, as you don't want to sound rehearsed. But certainly remember specific keywords you want to mention, and then the stories that build around them. Then practise it from memory, in front of a mirror. By doing this, you're already setting yourself apart from the majority of candidates who will employ the scatter gun approach, desperately scanning their own CV in their mind picking out bits and pieces here and there that they can remember. I've seen it happen. It's not a good way to start. Avoid that by being well-prepared.

On the next page, you'll find an example of a CV summary, based on the example CV in the previous section. Remember - 60 seconds or less!

Interviewer: "Can you give me a quick overview of your CV please?"/ "Tell me about yourself"/ "What's your background?"

John Smith: "So I just graduated from the University of Oxford this summer with a first in Economics and History. I was Sponsorship Officer for our University Help the Homeless charity in my first year, where I led a team to secure over £2,000 funding. This gave me a taste of how rewarding it can be to work towards and achieve a goal with a great team. In my second year I completed an 8-week internship at Silverman Sachs, where I was supporting transactions – including a live £300 million transaction - in the Mining & Metals team by putting together financial models. Although I learned a lot about finance and became a bit of a whizz at Excel, I wanted something more tangible to work on day-to-day. So a year later I completed an internship at The McBain Consulting Group, where I supported benchmarking and customer data analysis for a marketing project that eventually increased the client's marketing efficiency by 24%. I really loved the client exposure I got on this project and also being able to sink my teeth into a market and figure out not only how it works but how to beat it. I found it so rewarding that I'm now convinced that I want to move into consulting full time to really learn how to make businesses successful. I've got a real passion for the automotive industry in particular, and given Consulting Firm Ltd's automotive focus, I think it would be the perfect place for me to be."

CV BARBECUE

As an interviewer, the easiest direction in which to take an interview after the CV summary is by picking out individual experiences from the candidate's CV summary and asking for more detail. They might even pick an item on your CV that you didn't mention. This is to test the integrity of your CV. Have you put down some entries that sound impressive but were actually of very little value? Have you stretched the truth? What did you get out of your experiences? These are the questions going through the interviewer's head. I call this section the CV Barbecue, because you're getting a real grilling! Yep: unabashedly cheesy. Get over it.

As a top candidate, this is the perfect opportunity for you. After giving a taster of your experiences in the CV summary, this section is where you get to elaborate on those experiences. The interviewer could literally ask about any point you raised, or any point on your CV, so make sure you know everything you put down to the last detail. They might ask you about the team dynamics of the student committee you led, or the market model you worked on during your internship, or what the most valuable lesson was when you worked at an NGO. Know your own experiences inside out, back to front, so as to never to caught out by anything you're asked. Recite it in your sleep.

To prepare for this grilling, literally sit down with a pen and paper going through every item on your CV, writing backup material. And then write backup material for each point in your backup material. What I mean by backup material is detail to flesh out your main point. If you put a summer internship on your CV, prepare notes on the projects you were engaged in and the people you worked with. Then prepare notes on the successes/ failures of the project, what you learnt from it, and also the strengths and weaknesses you saw in the people who you worked with and who led you on the project. Then prepare notes on the experiences that led you to form those opinions on those people. If you're at the point where you've got two or three further levels of detail prepared for each and every item on your CV, you're absolutely laughing. At every stage of questioning, describe specifically the results of your achievements and mention how the experience helped you to become a person who is perfectly suited to consulting.

I VS WE

There is a bit of controversy about which pronoun you should use when describing your achievements: "I" or "we". Should you attribute achievements to yourself, the singular, or should you talk about the team? Did "I" increase membership by 20%? Did "I" manage to save the company from the brink of failure? Or did "we" do all that? On the one hand, the interviewer wants to know what you achieved. Not what other people who happened to be on the same team did. It's about the difference that you made to a situation, and how you handled difficulties. On the other hand you need to show that you are a team player, and give credit to others where it's due. Furthermore you need to be credible. Chances are you did not achieve things alone, and it would have been very difficult for any one person to do so. The best way to handle this is to use both for different situations. "We" managed to turn the society around from a loss-making situation, and "I personally" drove a marketing campaign that resulted in £4000 of donations", which contributed to the turnaround

MOTIVATION QUESTIONS

Motivations questions are pretty straightforward. They do exactly what it says on the tin: test your motivations for consulting, and for the company. Some examples questions:

- Why do you want to be a management consultant?
- Where do you see yourself in five years' time?
- If you couldn't be a consultant, what would you do instead?
- What do you hope to get out of a career in consulting?
- Why did you choose the degree you studied?

The key to answering these questions is to put yourself forward as an individual whose motivations make them ideally-suited to being a consultant. Characteristics such as being good at problem-solving, being passionate about business, being insatiably curious about different industries, wanting to work in a fast-paced, dynamic environment, and wanting to work alongside excellent individuals are all positive motivations for consulting. Not only should you mention these when asked why you want to work in consulting (which you should never be asked because you should have already mentioned it yourself!), but you should also have these at the ready for the questions about your alternative choices. When asked what you would do if you couldn't do consulting, don't pick something completely different. Choose a career that emphasises the same skills and characteristics. Same with why you studied your course. You want to show how consulting fits in perfectly with who you are as a person and what you want to achieve and experience in life. In short, you want to show that you have all the characteristics of a person who will thrive in consulting. Don't fall into the trap of talking too much about how much you'll enjoy the travel and the money. Talk, instead, about how you're motivated to move into a job you'll be very good at, and why you think you'll be very good at consulting. After all, they're not trying to hire the person who'll enjoy consulting the most. They're trying to hire the person who will be best at consulting.

FIT QUESTIONS

Fit questions, otherwise known as competency questions, are designed to see how well you'd fit into the team, and into the consulting profession. They're about testing your character and your personality rather than any particular skill. With a bit of preparation, the fit question could truly play to your advantage, as your answer can signal most of the characteristics we identified at the beginning of this book as being crucial for successful consultants.

A few examples of fit questions:

- What is your greatest strength?
- What is your greatest weakness?
- What makes you a good fit for consulting?
- Tell me about a time you led a team through a tough situation
- Tell me about a time you made a mistake
- How do you deal with conflict?
- Tell me about the biggest success you've experienced

These questions all have on thing in common: they invite you to tell a story. It's not good enough just presenting a situation in which you led a team, or admitting that you made a mistake once. It's about how you reacted to each situation, and what characteristics you demonstrated and what characteristics you developed. Characteristics that, of course, make you an excellent fit for consulting. The strengths and weaknesses questions may not look like they're inviting you to tell a story but they're just in disguise. As soon as you've mentioned what you think your biggest strength/weakness is, you should give an example of when you demonstrated/realised it. If you're talking about a weaknesses, do not finish the story until you've got to the bit where you learned from it and identified what you should be doing to improve.

The first step in preparing for fit type questions is to identify the stories you want to tell. There are only certain situations you could be asked about: working in a team, being a leader, facing adversity, making a mistake, being successful, improved an organisation, etc. You should draw up a table like the one on the next page, and match each of these situations to an item on your CV to which you can relate. You can have more than one per CV item, and can even use the same story to cover more than one situation, as long as it is genuinely suitable and not shoehorned in. The important thing is to ensure you have every situation covered so you're not left in the lurch when asked about it.

The ideal situation you want to be in is one where you have just three or four experiences which, combined, provide you with enough material to cover pretty much any fit type question/situation you could be asked about. So think about which of your experiences was the most diversely rewarding. Having to remember the specific details of just three experiences is much easier than having to remember seven!

FIT MATRIX	BEING A LEADER	DIFFICULT SITUATION	TEAMWORK	OTHERS...
MCBAIN CONSULTING GROUP INTERNSHIP		**1)** Client deliverable date moved forward by a week		*etc etc*
FINANCE SOCIETY PRESIDENT	**2)** Committee split when trying to decide the theme for conference	**3)** Needed to reprimand a committee member for shirking responsibilities		*etc etc*
NON-PROFIT ORGANISATION COMMITTEE	**4)** Was put in charge of temporary volunteers		**5)** Last-minute push to meet pitch-deadline for funding	*etc etc*
UNIVERSITY BASKETBALL TEAM		**6)** Conflict within the team when the 2013 line-up was announced		*etc etc*

Once you've identified the stories you want to tell, you then need to craft each story. A great framework for doing this is to use the STAR technique, which refers to an approach that is structured around Situation, Task, Action, Result:

Situation

Describe the situation to give the context for your story. What were you doing at the time? When did this experience take place? How many people were involved? Who were the main protagonists? What were the difficulties in the situation? What was your position in all this?

Task

Explain what your deliverable was – what did you need to accomplish, and what form did the result have to take? What were the constraints/conditions, if any? How closely your results matched the task you were given will be the benchmark for how successful the outcome was.

Action

Describe the action you, as an individual, took. Tailor this to the specific question you were asked to ensure you illustrate a picture that the interviewer is looking for. If the question was about dealing with conflict, don't talk about what a great job you did in marketing a product. Talk about the friction between your marketing team members and what you did to overcome that. This is the most important part of the whole story, as it illustrates the difference you would make to a situation. Ensure that you choose situations where the actions you took exhibit some of the seven qualities we talked about in the first section of the book!

Result

Finally, explain what happened as a result of your actions. Refer back to your original task to illustrate how successful you had been overall, and offer an explanation of what would have happened if you had not taken the action you took, to highlight the value you added to the situation.

You'll need to have a STAR structure for each of your stories, that you can just pull up from the back of your mind whenever you need to. Put together a table like the one on the next page and memorise it. It should include enough details so that you remember to include all the relevant points in your answer, but vague enough so that you won't memorise a passage of text and sound too rehearsed. You just need to be comfortable with the content and the message. All that's left to do is to identify which story you need to tell when you're asked a question. Then, if you're not too nervous, the rest will take care of itself.

STAR MATRIX	EXAMPLE STORY	*OTHERS...*
SITUATION	"I was elected President of the Finance Society, and the society ran an annual conference that was its flagship event for the year. A committee of eight members ran the society."	*etc etc*
TASK	"We ended up with two choices for the theme of the conference, and the committee vote ended in deadlock. We needed to decide as soon as possible as we had to actually put together the conference itself under intense time pressure. The theme was very important as it had to be engaging enough to attract as many attendees as possible."	*etc etc*
ACTION	"I had the casting vote, but I knew that I needed everyone on board so that the entire team would feel motivated to work towards the conference, rather than imposing a decision on the team. So I spoke with committee members individually to understand their specific objections to the other side's idea. I also called an emergency meeting that ran late into the night to properly debate the topic, raising each specific concern individually."	*etc etc*
RESULT	"After three days of discussions and some modification of the original ideas I called for a re-vote, where a very clear decision was taken by the committee. All but one person voted for the winning theme. We then worked extremely hard and pulled off a conference that pulled the largest audience in its history. I think that if I had made a firm decision straight away, I would have lost the support of half of my team, whereas if I had taken too long to act, we would have been too short of time to create a successful event."	*etc etc*

COMMERCIAL AWARENESS

Consulting firms want to hire someone who's passionate about business, and has a mindset that commercially-oriented. They want someone who already has a broad understanding of how markets work, how businesses operate, both from a theoretical perspective and practical realities. You need to understand what your clients are doing and why they do it. Only then can you start to think about what they could do better.

Commercial awareness isn't something you can get overnight. It's something that you build up over a period of weeks, months and years. Hopefully, being someone that's interested in consulting, you already have a decent dose of it. Commercial awareness questions can broadly be split into two categories: Principles of business and current affairs. It's important to keep in mind when answering questions of this type – and indeed all questions in your interview – that you still need to be structured in your approach. Just because the main focus of the question is on your commercial awareness, it doesn't mean you should start blabbering away. Keep composure. Always be structured.

Principles of Business

This is the bit that tests whether or not you're telling the truth when you say you're business-savvy. These questions test how well you know the business world and how it works. Things like what a private equity firm does, what the difference is between a private and public company, which are the major industries in the UK, relative size of industries, how an income statement is built, etc are all things you should know. But above and beyond specific tidbits of knowledge, you should have a good grasp of what business is, how it fits in with the world, what value a business adds, and the main channels through which that value can be increased. If all this is new to you, you'll have some serious work to do before you're able to answer questions such as:

- What makes a business successful?
- What are the symptoms of a failing business?

- What are the options available to a failing business?
- What's more important – business or government?
- What is a business?
- What challenges would a UK business have when looking to move expand abroad?

The way to be convincing with your answers to these questions is to have a common theme to all your answers that ensures you're being consistent. The way you see business and how it fits in with the rest of the world should inform your answers to all of these questions. For example, I personally believe that businesses exist to gather and reassemble resources in a way that makes people's lives better, and that while it has its shortcomings, the market system and the profit motive is the most efficient way in which humans know how to combine and distribute the limited resources we have. All this will inform what I believe makes a firm successful or not, and consequently inform what action can be taken to push a firm towards the right direction. Other bits of knowledge such as being able to create a cash flow and income statement are tools that facilitate action.

The way to prepare for this section is to read like your life depended on it. Primers on economics and business are a good start. There are also a multitude of great blogs and online columns to turn any layman into an informed individual in a matter of days. Get to it! Because even if you don't get asked these questions directly, being knowledgeable enough to answer them will show through in your analysis of questions in other parts of the interview.

Current affairs

You already read business news. Good. If that statement is not true, then rectify the situation. Forthwith. Being passionate about business and being interested in the business world means caring about what's going on in that world. Keep up to date on the biggest M&A deals currently under discussion, and the ones that have just completed. Has any company performed particularly well or badly over the last quarter? Know why. Has a significant piece of government legislation been introduced recently that will affect businesses? Have an opinion. Has there been any big product launches that have hit the press recently? Do you think it was successful? You won't get asked about current affairs in every interview, but they're always good to have in your mind even if they don't come up – certain topics might crop up in conversation and you'll be doing yourself a massive favour if you can offer a well-considered opinion. If you read publications such as the Financial Times, The Economist or the Wall Street Journal on a regular basis, you'll be well prepared for questions such as:

- What were the causes of the financial crisis of 2008?
- What are your thoughts on the current business climate in the UK?
- Which company would be a dream client for you right now?
- Which industries are doing particularly badly at the moment? Why?
- What are the key trends that will affect UK businesses in the next 5 years?
- What's going on in the music industry right now?
- What are the main benefits of the recent XYZ merger?
- What are the biggest challenges facing UK businesses today?

I'll be honest – not that many candidates will prepare for current affairs questions in detail, so be keeping up with the news you're already ahead. But to stand out from the other candidates that are as diligent as your are, have a well-considered opinion on the events that occur. Don't just regurgitate what you read in the article. Another piece of advice is to always address "why?" and, if appropriate, "so what?", even if not asked about it directly. For example, if asked "what's going on in the music industry?", a decent candidate will talk about how the business model is changing from one that was label-centric to one that is more fragmented and more focused on live music. A good candidate will explain that this has largely been due to the rise of the Internet enabling both convenient piracy of recorded media and the democratisation of music creation fostered by technological advances. A great candidate will go on to explore and assess some of the alternative business models that have emerged to try to deal with this trend (e.g. on-demand) and even present hypotheses for the key success criteria a new business model will need to address in order to thrive.

Remember: acquire the knowledge and then add your own analysis to it. It doesn't hurt to sound bloody passionate, too!

CONSULTING QUESTIONS

Consulting questions are ones that test your knowledge and opinions of the consulting industry, what a consultant does, and he specific firm to which you've applied. The interviewer is trying to work out how much you actually want to be a consultant. As in actually live the life of a management consultant, rather than conceptually want this great career everyone's told you so many awesome things about. And the first step to gauging whether or not you really want something is to figure out if you know what that something actually is.

These questions are a real easy win, because all you have to do is read up on it. If you've been diligent, then you'll have done it already. It should have been the first thing you did when you thought about going into consulting. Like I've been saying throughout this book – if you care enough about your future career, you should have done all the research you can into an industry that is likely to consume the next few years of your life. I can't drum this home enough. If you haven't done any research on what consulting is, or have an opinion on it by the time you walk into the interview, you're a real muppet. Even reading the first section of this book will give you a good primer on the industry! I'm going to presume you're not a muppet, and know what consulting entails. What you should then do is arrange that knowledge in your mind in a way that makes it easy for you to answer questions such as:

- What does a management consultant do?
- Why do firms hire consultants?
- Who are our main competitors?
- What makes our firm different to our competitors?
- Are consultants worth the money?
- Where do you see the consulting industry in 5 years time?

Remember – while you should be giving an accurate and honest opinion of what you think about the industry and the firm, they want to hire somebody who is enthusiastic and believes in the value they are bringing to clients. So it's probably not a great idea to go on a rant about how you think consultants are a terrible waste of money for the client. In any case, if you do hold that view then I don't know why you're applying in the first place.

Also it will serve you well to keep abreast of industry developments. Any M&A activity that's been going on? It would have been awfully silly to have been the Monitor candidate who was completely oblivious to the Deloitte deal in 2012/2013.

For bonus points, tie your answers in with your application and your motivations. Don't just list the reasons the firm is different to its competitors – tack on to the end of your answer the reasons that unique environment is one that will enable you to thrive in your career. All the benefits that a client might hope to realise when hiring consultants resonate very well with your professional values. Of course they do. That's why you'll make a great consultant.

ACING THE INTERVIEW:
THE CASE

So you've arrived at the case. You've heard of the case before, and you kinda know what it is: a test of your ability to solve a problem, on the spot, with no prior knowledge. It tests your ability to think on your feet, your business instincts, your basic maths, your ability to explain your reasoning and your ability to keep your cool. And above all else, do keep your cool. Once you lose that, you've lost everything. While you can fail an interview before you get to the case, you certainly can't pass one without giving a great performance in this section. I've seen a great number of candidates do very well until they get to the case. And to be honest with you it's not difficult to become good at cases. It's just a knack - a knack which anyone can get. This section of the book talks about what types of cases there are and how to approach each of them. There will also be solved examples as well as a number of unsolved examples for you to practise with your friends. And *do practise*. I'd say that this is the part that most candidates are weakest on, so spend as much time as you can on it as you can really differentiate yourself by being bloody brilliant at it.

BREAKING THE CASE

Cases are like mini-projects, really. They are the same kind of questions you'll be faced with when you're on a project working for a client. The only difference really is that there isn't much context, and you don't have any real data. However the principle is still the same: You are a given a problem and you need to work out the best way to solve it. The key word there is "solve". Notice how that doesn't say "answer". The interviewer is looking to see how you approach, structure and solve problems, and is far less interested in the final result. So when you get given a question, don't answer straight away. Take a bit of time to think about how you would solve it. The first thing you need to do is to work out what type of case it is. Once you've done that, you just have to run through the process.

There are three main types of cases that are given to entry-level candidates:

Market Sizing
- How many pairs of sunglasses are sold in the UK every year?
- How much money will billboard advertisers in the UK make this year?

Revenue and Cost
- Company X has noticed its profits are falling. Why?
- Company Y has just raised its prices. What is likely to happen?

Business Strategy
- Company A wants to expand into a new product line. What should it consider?
- Company B is losing market share. How should it respond?

In terms of frequency, I'd say roughly 50% of cases given are market sizing, 30% revenue and cost and 20% business strategy. Market sizing and revenue and cost cases are also a bit easier to solve as they are more predictable, while business strategy cases can vary a little more.

No matter what type of case you're given, you should approach it in the same, structured, considered manner. For every single case you'll ever come across, you should be disassembling the question and each component part of the problem until you can do so no more.

The first thing you should always do is the write down the question, word for word. Then double check it with the interviewer. Not only does this show that you're conscientious and detail-oriented, it actually helps you with the case! Firstly it buys you a little bit of time in which you can already start thinking about the question, and secondly it serves as a point of reference for checking later if you've answered the question. Ask any initial clarifying questions now before asking for a little bit of time (10-20 seconds or so) to identify the case and consider the question. The next section will run you through each of the three types of cases and how to approach them.

MARKET SIZING

Market sizing questions are always asking you to estimate a number for something. It might be profits/revenues for a company, it might be the number of motorcycle helmets sold in the UK, it might be number of golf balls that can fit inside Big Ben. Most of the time it will be a number for which you'd never know off the top of your head. You can't guess it. So don't try. You have to use rough assumptions to work it out. These questions are really popular since they're so easy for the interviewer to ask and assess. When I interview I often make up a market sizing case when I'm sat there asking it. I don't know what the answer is, and to be frank I don't care. What I care about is how you approach the question, how structured that approach is, how decent your maths is and how good you are at communicating your ideas and walking me through your logic. These questions are also a reflection of the type of work you'd do on a project, where calculating the size of a market is crucial to sizing up an opportunity for the client. The only difference is you'd have to follow through with real numbers.

So when you get hit with that question asking you to estimate the size of the beer market in the UK, don't panic. Calmly take your pen and write the question down at the top of the page. Then read it back to your interviewer to check that you've got it right. Ask any clarifying questions at this stage. Are we talking about on or off-licence? Both. And it's revenue I need to get to? Yep. Ok Cool. Can I just take a few seconds to think through the question? Sure thing. Thanks.

This is where you think about the approach you're going to take. The framework for solving market sizing questions is pretty simple: a tree diagram. Always use and draw a tree diagram. It's the best way to keep track of where you are in a case, and to show the interviewer how well-structured you are. You want to put your objective on the left hand side of the tree, and then keep breaking it down until you can break it down no longer.

Usually you'll end up reaching a few standard assumptions you'll need to make, such as UK population (sometimes broken down by age) along with estimates for market segment penetration. For example, you would start the tree diagram for the beer example case thus:

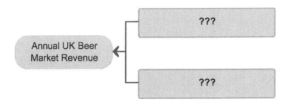

We want to arrive at the annual UK beer market revenue. How would we need to break it down? Well we know that revenue = price*quantity. So we could use that. But remember we're talking both on-licence, in bars/pubs etc, and off-licence, in shops. These different sales channels will have very different dynamics, so it's worth considering them separately. So you would develop your tree diagram like this:

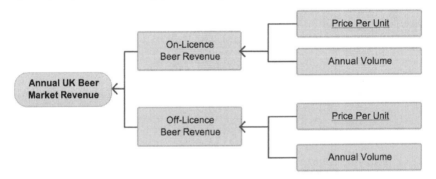

So now we've broken down the problem further and made it more manageable. Remember: whenever you see revenue, break it down into price and quantity! We'll have to estimate average prices for on- and off-licence beer sales, as well as annual sales volumes for each. Usually, you can't break down price assumptions any further, so it will just have to be an assumption you take from experience. It's good practice to keep track of your assumptions by underlining them so you can keep track of which channels your numbers are coming from and how they're affecting your final outcome. Anything that you can break down further, do so. In this case, we should break down annual volume:

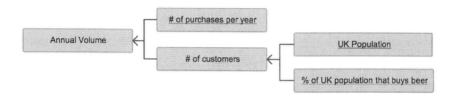

Once all of your inputs are at a stage where it would not be sensible to break them down any more because to break them down would be gibberish or you have a good estimate for that assumption, then you're finished with forming your approach. However, you need to judge the level of granularity required based on the context. One common example is that demand for many products is sensitive to either age or income, or both. In this case it would be a good idea to separate out segments for these factors before estimating the size of the market in each segment. For example, demand for beer is very sensitive to age - especially once you distinguish by on- and off-licence, so we should introduce age brackets to capture this sensitivity. The final tree diagram for this case is presented on the next page. Only two age segments are presented per sales channel for simplicity only. In reality you would use maybe four or five segments depending on the product.

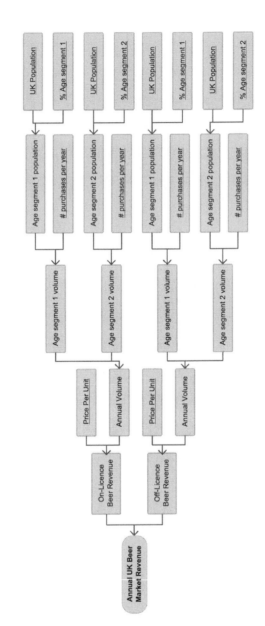

Now you've pretty much done it. All you need to do is to explain to the interviewer how you intend to solve the case (by walking them through your lovely tree diagram) and then execute on that! Go through each line step by step, making sensible numerical assumptions along the way and remembering which operator to apply, until you arrive at your answer. Then check that it answers the question you were asked in the first place. You've already written the question at the top of the page so it shouldn't be too difficult! Then sense-check the numbers. Are they silly? Do they imply that everyone in the country is a raging alcoholic? If not, you're probably ok.

Quite often at the end of a case, I'll ask the candidate what they think of their answer and why, no matter whether I think the number is way off or bang on target. This is just to test their common sense, and also their ability to pinpoint where potential errors are feeding into their analysis. For example if a candidate says that they think their answer was too high and I asked them why, the ideal response that would make me want to hire this candidate immediately would be to firstly do a top-down sense-check on the number (e.g. "this answer would imply that the UK spends on average £20,000 on beer per person per year, which is way too high considering average incomes in the UK") and then go through each raw assumption they made and make a call on which assumption it was that threw everything out. That implies a well-considered and reasoned approach to problem-solving rather than pure conjecture.

The assumptions you make during the case are the numbers that ultimately feed through to your final answer, and so the more accurate and precise they are the better. At worst you can always cite "personal experience" to make these assumptions, but where possible use proxies that are more accurate and reliable. For certain numbers such as average income, UK population, etc you should keep some standard numbers in mind, as they come in very handy in all sorts of cases.

The approach for all market sizing questions is pretty much the same as what I've laid out above. The trick is in choosing the best way to break down each node of the tree such that it's both accurate and easy to work with, and having sensible estimates for your raw assumption inputs. And remember - calculators are never allowed!

Finally, remember that every problem you get can be solved in two ways - top down and bottom up. With a top-down approach you're breaking a system down to gain insight into its component parts, while with a bottom-up approach you're piecing together smaller pieces in order to give you your final answer. It's worth noting that you can approach a case in either way, depending on which is easier. An example of the two different approaches to a single case is shown below: How many people visit UK aquariums per day? Both are simplified tree diagrams, for illustrative purposes only.

Aquarium Visitors: Top Down Analysis

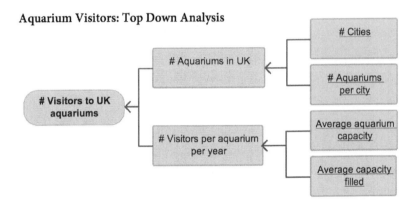

Aquarium Visitors: Bottom Up Analysis

TWO SIMPLE PHRASES

There are lot of websites out there with lists of "consulting phrases" that you apparently need to know to sound like you know your stuff. That's mostly rubbish. I don't care if you don't know what "on the beach" or "push back" means. One website even has "hands" and "hope you're doing well" in its glossary of consulting terms. Utter tripe. You don't need that stuff, and if I heard you word-dropping them in an interview it'll either make me chuckle to myself or put me off you completely, depending on how you were doing up that that point.

However there are two phrases that are actually useful during a market sizing interview, that are likely to crop up fairly often and would certainly earn you bonus points if I interviewed you. One is "penetration rate" and the other is "installed base". Why are these important? Well instead of just junk management speak, they refer to important concepts when assessing a market.

Penetration rate refers to the percentage of an overall market that purchases a product or service. For example, if we have a hundred people in a room and thirty of them buy fudge, then we'd say that the penetration rate of fudge is 30%. You can see how this is important - if I want to know how tubs of ice-cream are sold in the UK per year, then all I'd have to do is multiply the population by the penetration rate. Done. Easy.

Installed based refers to number of units that are already in use, as opposed to the number being sold. For example if you want to work out how much revenue a washing machine repair centre makes per year, you'd need to multiply the installed base by average annual repair cost. It's a much more elegant way of saying "the number of washing machines that people already own".

REVENUE AND COST

Revenue and cost cases are pretty self-explanatory. They require you to assess the revenues and costs of a company in order to solve a problem. Very often this will be a profit issue that you need to explore, but sometimes it will just be looking at either revenue or cost streams. No matter what it is, you just need the take the same approach.

Once again, write down the question and clarify it with your interviewer. Then, whip out this tree diagram below.

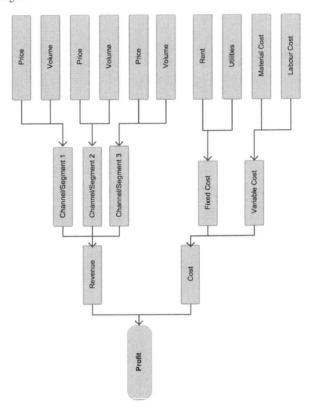

You should memorise this diagram. It's a classic. Kinda like Led Zeppelin IV. Then all you have to do is to go down each branch of the tree from left to right and diagnose where the problem is. For example if you're trying to work out why profit has fallen, then ask what's happened to revenues. Gone up? Ok, well in that case it must be a cost problem. What's happened to fixed costs? Etc etc. You get the idea. It's that simple. You go through each branch of the tree until you identify the problem. But remember just because you've found a cause in one branch doesn't meant that you've identified the whole problem - carry on through to completion.

INTERDEPENDENCIES, CAPACITY AND CANNIBALISATION

The only other thing you need to understand for revenue and cost cases is how different components within revenues and cost affect each other. For example if you prices go up, what happens? Well, assuming everything else stays the same your revenue will go up. However economics dictates that if price goes up, your demand will go down. If demand goes down, then variable costs will also go down.

So remember the relationship between **price, volume and variable cost**.

In certain industries you'll get a curveball, in the form of capacity. Capacity is how much a factory can produce at a given level of fixed cost. For example a bicycle factory may have a capacity of a hundred bicycles per year. That means that your volume can continue to grow and only affect variable costs up to an annual quantity of a hundred. After that you're at full capacity. That means that if you want to increase your quantity and sales, you'll have to incur the extra fixed costs of setting up a new factory. This isn't relevant in every case, but keep it in the back of your mind.

Cannibalisation refers to a reduction in sales revenue/volume of one product/sales channel as a result of an increase in another product/sales channel. For example if I sell bicycles from a shop right now, and introduce an online store where people can buy my bicycles, some of the guys who would have come into my shop will now buy online, thereby cannibalising my own sales. Again, this isn't that common in case studies by keep it in mind just in case it does because it's sure to impress if used correctly.

BUSINESS STRATEGY

These are the most varied of all the cases. You could get any type of question, from marketing to new market entry to competitive response. You can't bluff this one - it relies on you actually having given a hoot about business prior to the interview, and know about how to assess a business situation. That said, the general principle for a business strategy case is identical to that for market sizing and revenue and cost cases: deconstruction. Take what it is you need to analyse and keep on breaking it down until you have simple component parts that you can assess one by one. Once you have assessed all the parts, then synthesise to come up with a result.

Just like with any other type of case, you want to first write down the question and clarify any details with the interviewer. The approach you take then depends on what type of case you're given. The next few pages present the frameworks you should turn to first for a whole host of business strategy cases. If you get familiar enough with these frameworks that you can play with them in the palm of your hand, you'll be sorted for any possible variation or combination. Remember to always be flexible depending on the case you're given! It's impossible for me to illustrate every single type of business strategy case you could possibly get, so just get familiar and practise as much as you can!

Assessing a market

Certain questions need you to assess a market. These could be about entering/exiting a new market, producing a new product, or purchasing a company in a different market. For these questions, your first point of reference should be the very well-known **Porter's Five Forces** model. This assesses a firm's environment - the playing field, as it were. If the playing field is extremely unfavourable, you don't want to be playing the game. In order to conduct a Five Forces analysis, you must consider the power of suppliers and customers (usually based on how many there are - the fewer exist the more power they have), threat of new entrants and substitutes, and the competitive rivalry within the market. For each of these factors, assess weather the threat is high or low, and then aggregate the analysis to make a call on weather or not the market is an attractive one.

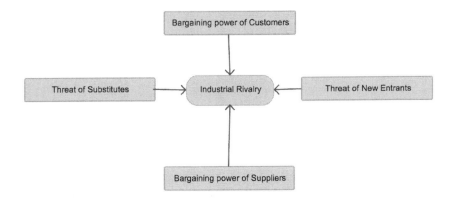

Assessing a firm/asset

There are a couple of options for assessing a firm or an asset. The most famous is perhaps **SWOT analysis** - Strengths, Weaknesses, Opportunities and Costs. It's literally a case of writing these four things down on a piece of paper and trying to think of the main items that can fall into each bucket. Dead simple.

SWOT ANALYSIS	HELPFUL	HARMFUL
INTERNAL	Strengths	Weaknesses
EXTERNAL	Opportunities	Threats

Then there are the **Three Cs** - Company, Customers and Competition. These are often the most critical factors when considering a firm's chances of making money. Once again, just write down the three Cs, and start assessing strengths and weaknesses for each one. If you're looking at a specific opportunity for a firm, think about what will change under each of the Three Cs if the firm were to pursue that opportunity.

Finally, in the case of M&A type cases, you obviously need to talk about **synergies**. In what areas will the two firms gel so well that they will join to become greater than the sum of their component parts?

Marketing

Marketers all know of the **Four Ps** - Product, Price, Promotion and Placement. These are the four main tools a marketer has in his toolkit when trying to market a product. Product refers to everything about the product itself, its features and the market it caters to. Price refers to retail/wholesale pricing, discounts, and other offers. Promotion is what people traditionally think of as marketing - things like advertising etc. Placement refers to the distribution channels of the product - where will it be sold and how will it be positioned?

International Expansion

For any questions relating to international expansion, you need to consider the differences between the firm's current country of operations and the target country. For this, the **CAGE Distance Framework** is ideal. The CAGE Distance Framework is used to assess Cultural Distance, Administrative Distance, Geographic Distance and Economic Distance. Each one of these measures of distance should be used to compare the similarities and differences between the two countries. Cultural Distance refers to language, social differences, Administrative Distance refers to differences in governance, currency and trade ties. Geographic Distance encompasses everything that involves physical characteristics - infrastructure, physical distance, travel requirements etc. Finally, Economic Distance refers to the similarities and differences in factors such as wealth, income and availability of financing. Consider how these factors would affect the attractiveness of an international expansion opportunity? How would they affect the strategy for approaching the deal?

General

In addition to the frameworks laid out above for considering specific scenarios, there are a number of approaches that are worth thinking about in all situations. Furthermore, they are there to act as a framework of last resort if you really can't decide what sort of case you've been given. They're incredibly simple, but also incredibly flexible.

Firstly, a useful dichotomy can be struck between **Internal and External Factors.** Can be applied to pretty much any situation where a firm is involved. Internal Factors include a company's capabilities, size, management, etc, while External Factors refer to competitor activities, economic considerations and industry trends. Businesses strategies where there is a close fit between a firm's internal factors and the external environment are likely to be the most successful.

The next approach is a very basic **Cost Benefit Analysis**. Literally making a list of all the costs and all the benefits of conducting an activity, and then at the end assessing whether the costs outweigh the benefits or vice versa.

Knowledge of **Supply and Demand** is crucial. Not to solving every case, but to understanding business and to working in consulting. As prices go up, demand goes down and supply goes up. As prices go down, demand goes up and supply goes down. If more supply is introduced, prices will go down, while higher demand will induce higher prices. These are the basics of how a market works and if you're not already familiar with this, I suggest you get familiar.

Last but not least, pretty much anything can be assessed with a **2x2 Matrix**, which is just a fancy way of saying a table with two columns and two rows. You can put whatever you like on each axis, and it can neatly segment any market for you. For example if we want to look at which markets in a country are the most attractive, we can draw up a 2x2 matrix comparing size and growth rate:

	SMALL MARKET	BIG MARKET
FAST GROWING	High Potential	Very Attractive
STAGNANT	Dud	Mature

Depending on which quadrant the various markets fall into, we can assess their characteristics and overall attractiveness. The key to using 2x2 Matrices is selecting appropriate axes. With the right selection, they can be used to analyse pretty much anything.

Remember that just knowing these frameworks is not enough. You need to practise enough cases to get familiar with when and how to use them. These frameworks are mainly just a way to assist you in thinking about the problem, and under many circumstances you'll also need to combine frameworks to solve certain cases. Learning the frameworks off by heart is a start, but no substitute for being able to accurately assess a business case through robust analysis and commercial flair. Whatever you do to answer the question, make sure that there is rhyme and reason to it. Break everything down into manageable chunks and then aggregate it again once you've analysed everything. Never dive in without a plan.

There are a number of cases for you to practise on at the end of this chapter.

MECE

The MECE (pronounced "meesee") principle is an important one. It's a concept that McKinsey places a lot of emphasis upon and means "mutually exclusive and collectively exhaustive". It is a grouping principle for separating a set of items into subsets, and stipulates that between the subsets there should be no overlap, and that they should cover everything. It is important for your case interview, as at each level of your tree diagram, the items should be covering everything, but not repeating anything. So avoid embarrassment by ensuring that your analysis is MECE!

For example if you were to categorise people by year of birth, that would be MECE assuming all birth years are known. However to do so by nationality would not be MECE because nationalities are neither mutually exclusive (some people have more than one) nor collectively exhaustive (some people have none). As a result, you'd end up double-counting some people and missing out others.

A NOTE ON NUMBERS

To successfully crack a case, you have to be good with numbers, and especially mental maths. That takes practice, practice and practice, and I shan't cover it here. There are plenty of books and websites that specialise in training your skills in mental arithmetic. You want to be at the point where adding, subtracting, multiplying and dividing numbers in your head is second nature. Taking percentages is particularly useful. Chances are you knew this already. So here's something you probably didn't know:

One top tip that I came up with when I was interviewing and I share with everyone who asks me for tips, is to familiarise yourself with working with the number twelve – it can make the process of calculating numbers in your case interview a lot less stressful.

The decimal number system to which we're accustomed is based on the number ten, so everything to do with ten is easy. Multiplication and dividing by ten is a breeze. However, ten is divisible by only five and two (excluding one, and itself). That means that if you try to divide any other single digit number, your calculation will get a bit more difficult. Twelve, on the other hand, is divisible by six, four, three and two – twice the number of numbers that ten is divisible by, making it easier to work with in twice as many situations.

How does this apply to a case study? As we've seen above, you'll often have to take proportions of numbers on your way to your final result. For example if five hundred cars have their tyres changed once every six years, you'll have to divide five hundred by six to work out how many have their tyres changed per year. You will not have a calculator, so the accuracy of your mental arithmetic is paramount. You'll have much less of a headache if your numbers worked out as nice round numbers as opposed to irrational numbers that you then had to work with. The more of a pain the maths becomes, the more likely it is you will get distracted from the rest of the case, and losing your structure becomes more of a danger. The table on the next page shows how much nicer twelve is to work with than ten when taking proportions.

	BASE 10	BASE 12
1/2	5	6
1/3	3.333333	4
1/4	2.5	3
1/5	2	2.4
1/6	1.666667	2
1/7	1.428571	1.714286
1/8	1.25	1.5
1/9	1.111111	1.333333

While using base 10 gives you four horrible numbers, using base 12 only gives you two horrible numbers. That's half the number of horrible numbers. And nobody likes horrible numbers.

You will only benefit from using base twelve if you get to choose your own assumptions at the start of the case, which you often will be able to. The general rule is that for the largest number assumption (e.g. population), choose the closest sensible number that is divisible by twelve. This is the number you're most likely to have to divide by other number assumptions. And then for other number assumptions, try to avoid sevens and nines. You may not understand this immediately, but once you try a few cases with it you'll be laughing. This tip won't make you a maths genius, but it can just make things a little easier.

On the subject of numbers, it's a good idea to keep a few standard numbers in mind to pull up during a market sizing case. If you're asked to estimate the number of computers sold in the UK every year, it would be useful to know the number of people who live in the UK. I'd recommend knowing the rough populations of major economies and of London, average life expectancy and income in the UK, etc. And of course if you can get away with it, approximate to a number that's divisible by twelve!

BREAKING THE CASE IN 7 STEPS

1. Write down the question, and double check it with the interviewer

2. Identify the case as a market sizing, business operations or business strategy

3. Take some time to gather your thoughts and remember the right framework for solving the case

4. Explain to the interviewer what your approach is going to be

5. Execute on that approach, thinking out loud and writing down every step and ensuring that your maths is accurate - clarify where you make assumptions and where they come from

6. Before you give your final answer, check that it matches the question you were given

7. Perform a sense check - is your number really wacky, or does it look ok?

SOLVED CASE EXAMPLES

1. Market Sizing Case Example

Interviewer: *Please can you estimate the size of the pizza market in the UK?*

Candidate: *Sure. I presume we're talking about the end consumption market rather than wholesale?*

Interviewer: *That is correct*

Candidate: *And by "size", I guess we're talking about annual revenue?*

Interviewer: *Yep*

Candidate: *Ok, let me just take a moment to figure out how I'm going to tackle this....so for revenue we need price and quantity, and I know that pizza is sold both in shops for home consumption and in restaurants. Oh, I suppose we also have the takeaway pizza segment. So I'll have to break the market down into these three segments:*

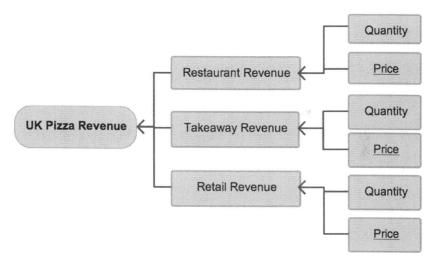

Candidate: *So for each of these segments I'll have to establish quantity and price. For price I'll go from experience...At a normal restaurant, pizzas cost on average £12 I'd say. For takeaway*

they're usually £8, and to buy them frozen we're talking about something really cheap - like £3. Let me just write these down to use later...

Interviewer: *How are you going to deal with quantity?*

Candidate: *Well pizza is bought many times a year, so I'll have to work out how often each one is bought, and by how many people. Firstly, I think that propensity to buy pizza through each channel depends on income, so I'm going to split the UK population into several income brackets, and estimate how often people in each income bracket buy pizza through each channel per year. Then I'm going to estimate how many people are in each income bracket and multiply it through to get quantity for each sales channel. Finally I'll multiply prices through and add them all together to reach overall size of the pizza market in the UK. Does that sound reasonable?*

Interviewer: *Absolutely.*

Candidate: *Great, so firstly let's look at number of pizzas bought per year by income...pizzas bought in shops aren't very nice and are really cheap, so I'm going to assume that students and those on low-income are the biggest consumers of those. Takeaway pizzas are seen as quite a standard convenient option for a lot of people, but in particular young professionals. Pizza you get at a restaurant can be pretty nice and given the higher cost I think that those on higher incomes will consume more. So I think that the picture for number of pizzas bought each year by the average person in each income bracket would correspond to the table I've drawn:*

INCOME VS SALES CHANNEL	RESTAURANT	TAKEAWAY	RETAIL
0-20K	0	10	20
20-40K	5	20	10
40-60K	7	10	5
60-80K	7	3	0
80K+	7	0	0

Candidate: *The UK has a population of about sixty million people, and they're probably distributed along the income spectrum like this:*

INCOME DISTRIBUTION	# PEOPLE
0-20K	7 million
20-40K	35 million
40-60K	10 million
60-80K	6 million
80K+	2 million

Candidate: *If I multiply through, that means that every year in the UK, 301 million pizzas are bought in restaurants, 888 million are bought from takeaways and 540 million are bought from retail outlets. If I then multiply the prices through, we're looking at a market size of.... £12.34 billion. That seems really high*

Interviewer: *Why do you say that?*

Candidate: *Well that would imply that everyone in the UK spends about £200 on pizza per year on average...it doesn't seem quite right.*

Interviewer: *Where do you think the error was introduced?*

Candidate: *Well let's see...I think the prices are pretty accurate, so it must be quantity. What did I get here...301 million pizzas in restaurants, 888 million from takeaways and 540 million from shops...that's almost 2 billion pizzas between 60 million people...that's like 30 pizzas a year per person! That's far too high.*

Interviewer: *Yes, I think you're probably right about that.*

Candidate: *The actual number is probably half that much, if not even less.*

Interviewer: *Our client is the UK's largest producer of pasta, and they've brought us in because their profits have been falling this year. What do you think has happened?*

Candidate: *Well profit is comprised of revenue and cost components. Let's look at each one...why has profit been falling? Have revenues fallen? Have costs increased?*

Interviewer: *Both have happened actually. It's a really sticky situation...*

Candidate: *Oh right. Well let's dig a bit deeper into each one, in that case. I've just drawn this diagram to make sure that I cover everything*

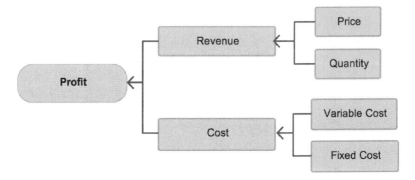

Candidate: *So what's been happening to prices?*

Interviewer: *They've been reduced recently - the client has been been trying to sell more to boost revenue*

Candidate: *And I'm guessing that hasn't worked?*

Interviewer: *Well it has actually - quantity has increased of late*

Candidate: *But overall revenue has fallen, which means that demand must be quite inelastic - demand can't have increased THAT much...otherwise revenue would increase*

Interviewer: *Correct. Quantity has only gone up marginally*

Candidate: *What about costs then? If quantity has increased then variable costs must have gone up too. Have fixed costs been increasing?*

Interviewer: *No - they've not moved.*

Candidate: *Ok, so we've better have a closer look at variable costs. Variable cost is quantity multiplied by cost per unit. We know that quantity has increased slightly, but it doesn't sound like it's that significant...it must be cost per unit. Have our raw material prices been going up?*

Interviewer: *Yep - the price of flour has hit the roof recently*

Candidate: *That'll explain it. And just in case...what about labour?*

Interviewer: *No, labour prices haven't budged at all*

Candidate: *Ok, in that case I think that the falling profits was mainly caused by the increasing price of flour - most likely due to a bad harvest. It's not been helped by cutting prices, but given that all of our client's competitors will have faced the same cost increase, I don't think it's a significant threat to long term performance.*

3. Business Strategy Case Example

Interviewer: *You work for a company that sells microscopes. It's the second largest player in the market and it is losing market share. What options do we have?*

Candidate: *Ok, well firstly I need to work out why we're losing market share. Are we losing market share by volume or by revenue?*

Interviewer: *Both. Proportionally.*

Candidate: *In that case I presume our prices haven't changed, so it sounds like our loss of revenue share is volume driven?*

Interviewer: *That's correct*

Candidate: *Ok, so I need to look into why our volumes are falling while our competitors' volumes are not. I presume this is a marketing problem rather than a production problem - we've not had any capacity constraints, have we?*

Interviewer: *Nope - our production lines are running smoothly*

Candidate: *So we're making enough microscopes, we're just not selling enough - that definitely sounds like marketing to me. Let's split this problem up first and see what's going on with us internally, and then what's going on externally in the market in terms of marketing issues. So there are a few things we should look at. We've already established that prices haven't changed - is true across the board? No new discounts have been offered or anything?*

Interviewer: *Nope - all prices have remained static.*

Candidate: *Right, what about our competitors?*

Interviewer: *Some have reduced prices, others have stayed the same.*

Candidate: *Ok, so there's some movement there. I imagine falling prices are eating into our volume share a bit. What about product? Has our product changed recently?*

Interviewer: *Nope - we're still selling the same things we did a couple of years ago*

Candidate: *And what about the market? Has anything new come along?*

Interviewer: *Yes, actually - one of our competitors released a new type of microscope a few months ago. It performs a little better than ours but we're not that worried because it's just one company, and they can't make that many units to compete with us anyway. Plus the company is spending so much on advertising they're going to run out of cash soon.*

Candidate: *I see. So we've got a new product on the market that's at the same price point as ours, performs better, and is better advertised?*

Interviewer: *Well, yes but only temporarily. Anyway it's not even sold that well*

Candidate: *Well I think I know what's going on, but in the interests of being MECE, has anything changed by way of distribution channels?*

Interviewer: *No, nothing*

Candidate: *Ok, so I think I've identified the problem. We've got a new product on the market that's a bit of a threat - it performs better than what's already out there and costs the same. While it might be a temporary blip, a lot of our competitors are scared so they've reduced their prices on products in a similar category to ours, and because of the price difference they're now selling better than we are. So it's not the new snazzy product that's taking our market share, but the fact that the other guys have all dropped their prices because they're afraid of this thing.*

Interviewer: *That sounds very plausible. What do you think we should do?*

Candidate: *Well in the long run it sounds like this new product is pretty strong, and given that the guys making it today are tiny, I think there's an opportunity for us to use that new technology to become the dominant player. I suppose our options are to purchase that smaller company or conduct our own research to obtain the technology. Obviously the make a firm call on that I'd need to do some further analysis. How profitable is this small company?*

Interviewer: *It's ok let's leave that for now. What should we do in the short run?*

Candidate: *Well the obvious decision we have to make is whether or not we drop our prices too. To inform that decision I'd need to conduct margin analysis to figure out what it's likely to do to profits. Furthermore, I'd want to know more about our brand and how we're perceived in the market, and how a price drop could affect that.*

Interviewer: *Great. Let's follow up with that another time. Thanks.*

MORE PRACTICE CASES

1. How many laptops are sold in the UK every year?

2. How much revenue did the AA make in 2012?

3. Our company's sales volumes are increasing and costs are falling. But our profits are plummeting. What's going on?

4. Estimate the number of people in the UK who own a ukulele

5. Company A prints books. How do you expect it has performed in the last few years?

6. How many bottles of single malt whisky left Scotland in 2012?

7. A boutique Swiss watch company is considering expanding into Asia. What should it consider before doing so?

8. What is the size of the market for car insurance in the UK?

9. How much revenue did the plumbing industry make in the UK in 2012?

10. How many national lottery tickets were sold last week?

11. How many people in the UK have never left the country?

12. A map-making company is considering a move into delivering parcels. What factors should it consider?

13. Company B's prices have fallen. What do you expect to happen?

14. What is the size of the fixed line telephone market in the UK?

15. A company selling digital cameras is losing market share. You've been brought in to solve the problem. What's going on?

ACING THE INTERVIEW:
AFTER THE CASE

QUESTION AND ANSWER

At the end of pretty much every single interview, you will get the chance to ask questions to the interview. This is a great opportunity to find out a few things about the firm, the industry, the job and the lifestyle that perhaps you were unable to find out so far. What most candidates tend to forget, however, is that they are still in the interview. Your assessment is not yet over: the questions you ask and how you respond to the answers still count towards your overall performance in the interview, so don't let go just yet.

What kind of questions should you be asking, then? Sure, there are questions that you're interested in: how much will you be paid? How much holiday will you get? Will you be expected to travel? Will you have to get up really really early? And these are all valid things about which you'd be right to be curious. However, they're pretty blah. Best case scenario, your interview will tell you the answers and forget about the whole thing. More likely they'll remember you as the guy/girl who asked some pretty useless questions, and there's a chance you'll be seen as caring too much about the money, thinking about taking time off already, and hoping to slack off.

The questions you ask at end of the interview reveal your priorities. If you ask about money first, the interviewer will presume that's what you care about most. Therefore the type of questions you want to ask are those that not only will give you information you care about, but also serve a signalling purpose - they reveal your priorities: priorities that indicate you will make a great consultant. Details such as salary, holiday arrangements, lifestyle can all be ironed out after you get an offer, when the firm will be trying to woo you as much as they can. In the meantime, focus on presenting yourself as an ideal candidate.

And if your priorities are in the right place, the questions that present you well are the very ones you should be concerned about anyway.

So what kind of questions should you ask? Remember consulting firms want to hire those candidates who are passionate about business and hungry for success. Think about what really matters to your long term development and success within consulting, and within the wider business world - once you've done so, then a whole host of questions should come to mind. A few of them might be:

- What's the training scheme like?
- What were the most important things you learned in your first year as a consultant?
- If you could give any piece of advice to yourself when you started in consulting, what would it be?
- What are the top mistakes made by new consultants?
- What are the three things I should be aiming to master immediately in order to succeed in this firm?
- Where do you see the consultancy industry in five years' time?
- What's the most difficult part of your job?

Just as I've been emphasising throughout the rest of this book: it's no use just memorising the above questions, noting down the answer and then moving on. If you're not actually interested in the answer, the interviewer can tell. You need to actually care about the training regime - is it going to train you as rigorously as the other firms you're applying to? You need to genuinely want to know what mistakes to avoid once you enter the consulting world. I can't stress this enough - if you're the kind of person who genuinely cares about these issues, you're the kind of person who will get in and will thrive in the consulting environment.

So remember: think hard about what your priorities are for your career, and ask questions that signal those priorities. Finally, if you genuinely care about these issues, chances are you'll have thought about them already. So be prepared for the interviewer to throw the question straight back at you, before providing his or her answer. Have a considered opinion and don't get caught out!

CONCLUSION

That's it. You're all done. Shake hands, thank your interviewer, and leave. Chances you got their business card. Should you send a thank you note to follow up? Probably not. I've never known it to make the slightest bit of difference during recruiting. However, following up on something that was discussed during the interview is a plus – especially if it's not forced. If you discussed a particular industry that both you and the interviewer are interested in during the interview, then absolutely do send through that interesting article you just read on the topic. If you get through to the next round, then it's also a good idea to ask your previous interviewer for where you can improve for the next one. They liked you enough to put you through, so chances are they'll be very happy to give you any help you need to go even further.

INTERVIEW CHECKLIST

1. Memorise your CV summary – a sub-60-second rundown of your education and experience, what you got out of it, and how that fits with consulting
2. Have a clear story for why you want to pursue a career in consulting, and with the specific firm to which you've applied
3. Prepare a handful of experiences you can call upon for any competency question and memorise all the details
4. Prepare for the case – learn the frameworks you need and when to use them; prepare some standard input numbers
5. Questions for the interviewer – prepare intelligent questions that reveal your priorities to be well-placed

Note: This checklist is something to think about in the days leading up to an interview. It assumes that you've already gone and done the really important stuff, like learning how to be structured, set your mentality to focus on results, become passionate about business, and all that kind stuff. It also helps if you're a pleasant person to deal with, but I didn't think that was appropriate for a checklist, since if it's not covered then there's not much you could do. Good luck.

EPILOGUE:
NAILING THE FIRST FEW WEEKS

So you've reached the end of the book. Apologies for the cliché, but this doesn't mean your preparation is finished. It means you can begin. I know that sounds incredible cheesy, but it's true. Now you know what you need to prepare for, so go and do it. If you're super-keen, you'll have a set of lovely index cards by the time your first interview rolls around, reminding you of all the things you need to have memorised when you step through that door. If you've really absorbed everything I've written and prepared accordingly, I'd have a hard time turning you away after interviewing you. Of course, you'd also have to not choke up in the interview.

So assuming all went well....Congratulations! You've broken into consulting. Now the fun begins. Remember all those projects you said you'd love to do? All those industries you wanted to see? All the clients you wanted to help? Well now you have to deal with all of it. And you want to hit the ground running.

The most important point to remember when you first start is your objective for the first few weeks: to rapidly become an independently valuable member of a case team. That means getting to the point at which you can be handed a piece of analysis to do and be trusted to be able to do it without too much hands-on guidance. When a fresh graduate joins, they add very little value outside of conducting basic research. Generally, if a fresh consultant makes a slide deck or builds a piece of spreadsheet analysis, someone else will have to rebuild it before it can be shown to a Partner or a client. That's the expectation. That will be a period of time that applies to you, just as it has applied to every new consultant before you. Your objective is minimise the amount of time you spend in that zone. You claimed to be a fast learner during the interview process: now is the time to prove it. After weeks and weeks of preparing for the interviews, some new joiners will be tempted to relax once they start the job. After all, you've done it! You've reached your objective. Except the real game is just beginning. Literally. And the first few weeks are when you make your reputation in the office. Consulting work couldn't be more different to university assignments, so spend any spare time you get looking at exemplar market models and client presentations to learn exactly what it is you should be aiming for, and then aim for it. Learn to make your presentation slides "client ready" before handing them in, even if it takes a little longer. Check and recheck your numbers before they go out, and then do it all over again. You want to become zero defect. The quicker you get there, the quicker you'll be recognised as someone who can be trusted to get work done to a high standard, and the more responsibility you'll be given.

Furthermore, stay as hungry and enthusiastic as you were during the application process. You probably would have killed to get the chance to grab coffee with a consultant when you were applying for a job. You should keep the same mentality. Except now, all your colleagues are consultants! So take any opportunity you get to chat with them about how things work in the office, how your firm conducts certain activities and get all the tips you can about how to get ahead in the first few weeks and months. You'll get some great insights, and also show yourself to be a dedicated member of the team who is constantly looking for ways to improve.

Just as important as the work is the social life. When I asked an interviewer for his top tip for a new consultant, he said to make friends. Everyone around you has been through the same rigorous process you've just been through. They're all brilliant people. They'll be able to help you no end when you're new, and you'll be able to help each other in ten years' time when you're all in much higher-up positions than you currently are. They'll end up spreading themselves all over the world in all sorts of companies and industries, and having that network will be one of the best things you get out of consulting, even if you don't stay in the job that long.

Finally, be likeable! Especially when you're on the client site. On your first client-facing case, you could be tempted to shy away from attention. After all you're the junior member of the team who probably has the least to add. Try not to give in to this temptation.

One of the best things you can do when you first see a client is to prove to your colleagues that you're comfortable in client communication. Obviously don't butt in every three minutes just to make your voice heard, but if you have something to add to a discussion, then don't be shy in voicing your thoughts. The client is the one paying everyone's salary, so if they like you, then you're golden. However, the flip-side is also true. If you're hated by the client, there's little anyone can do for you, even if you're well-liked by your colleagues and superiors. At the end of the day, you're there to serve the client and make them happy.

Anyway, you're now more than on your way towards a cracking career. Just keep doing what you've been doing to make yourself excellent. My final word of advice would be this: constantly review your overall career/life objectives, and ask yourself how your current job fits in with that. Work out how you need to develop to get to where you want to get to, and when the time comes, don't be afraid to recognise that maybe you need to move on.

ACKNOWLEDGEMENTS

I don't think this book is genuinely significant enough to warrant an Acknowledgements page. However, in its creation I have become indebted to a number of people, and that consideration alone is more than enough to convince my better judgment to acquiesce. Some of those people are mentioned below.

Brigadier General Uri Bram was the chief influence for this book. Without his inspiration, guidance, and cheerleading, I would never have started writing. Nine words at the end of his first book led to five thousand or so at the start of mine.

The last five thousand words would have never been written if not for the encouragement and admonition I received from Jiajia. It's safe to say that if not for her this book would never have been finished, instead having fallen victim to the perennial foe that is procrastination.

I am eternally grateful to two people who accepted me into the world of management consulting and have given me unfailing support ever since. One is Joanna Melewska. The other knows who he is.

I had intended to use the first book cover I designed for this. Robert Phipps told me off, so I designed another one. I much prefer the new one. Thanks Rob.

Michael Dent, Director at Liberty Tech, is something of a corporate sponsor, which entitles him to a mention here also.

Much love and gratitude go out to my parents for putting up with a son who has ideals and aspirations beyond his station and his abilities.

Finally, an enormous "cheers mate!" to Mark Spillman, whose ready supply of Analytical Grade ethanol made all the difference.

http://www.breaking-entering.com

Printed in Great Britain
by Amazon